"*Reflections of a Schoolmistress* opens the door to a rare view of American life in the late ninteenth and early twentieth centuries. Nora Frye defies easy generalization. Small town or big city in Europe or in America, here was a keen observer of life, someone who enjoyed the world she found.

Nora Frye's midwestern farm origins and her many teaching appointments in small town schools made her a part of those worlds. She was at home with and happy with small town rural America. For her, the banker, the minister, the principal, as well as the farmers and the local characters, were all part of a pageant set out to be observed. If her stories and reminiscences remind the reader of Edgar Lee Masters' *Spoon River Anthology*, they have none of Masters' preoccupation with the bitter-sweet and the maudlin. Nora Frye saw dignity and generosity, not to mention gaiety and humor, in rural America. Her world was not sugar-coated—there was disappointment and tragedy—but the people she described were not victims, nor were they ridiculous. This said, Nora Frye never took herself too seriously either. Her stories reflect her understanding and her values, but they do not moralize.

This book would be valuable and interesting were it only to describe small town life in midwestern America. However, Nora Frye occupied a wider world. Several of her stories and many of her letters describe her trip to Europe in 1923. She enjoyed Europe to the full—the cities, the countryside, the galleries, the cathedrals—but she was never awestruck. Her observations are insightful and self-deprecating. For all of its beauty and interest, Europe was not perfect. Having absorbed what she liked, she was happy to leave the London of T.S. Eliot and the Paris of Ernest Hemingway and return home. We get a very balanced view of an American abroad.

Nora Frye also gives us a brilliant view of New York in 1937. Once again the small town woman broke out of any stereotype and plunged with gusto into the settlement house work of New York in the Great Depression. We benefit from her compassionate but unsentimentalized view of urban America.

It is delightful to find that Nora Frye's life touched, if briefly, some of the famous, here again defying any stereotypical small town image. Her portraits of Maria Sanford and Vachel Lindsay are wonderful and are revealed here for the first time.

Given the diversity of Nora Frye's experience, we see a rich and remarkable view of American life."

Francis Carroll, B.A. Carleton College; M.A. University of Minnesota; Ph.D. Trinity College Dublin; Professor of History, St. John's College, University of Manitoba; 1994-95, John Adams Fellow, Institute of United States Studies, University of London. He is the author of five books, including: *Crossroads in Time: A History of Carlton County, Minnesota*. With Franklin R. Raiter, *The Fires of Autumn: The Cloquet-Moose Lake Disaster of 1918*.

REFLECTIONS
OF A SCHOOLMISTRESS

by
Nora Frye

Compiled and Edited by Janet Schultz Panger

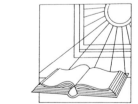

AURINKO PUBLICATIONS

St. Cloud, Minnesota 56304

International Standard Book Number 0-9643799-0-2

Manufactured in the United States of America

10 9 8 7 6 5 4 3 2 1

Library of Congress Catalog Card Number 94-79184

Cover photo: Nora Frye, 1916

To order a single copy of this book, send $10.95 (plus .065% sales tax for Minnesota
residents), plus $3.00 for postage and handling to Aurinko Publications, 1412
Eighth Avenue S.E., St. Cloud, Minnesota 56304. Postage for additional copies,
$.75 each.

To all of the descendants
of Daniel Lee Frye
and Sarah Graffam Frye

Foreword

The writing of Nora Frye speaks, perhaps more eloquently than any of the recollections of those who knew her, of a life dedicated to teaching, but even more to being a life-long learner. Her zeal for new experiences and acquaintances shines through all of her writing. Her disclaimer that she wrote "just for fun" belies a perceptive skill which is captured both in her letters and in her essays.

Nora's interest in the people around her makes her vignettes fascinating observations of everyday life. These snapshots are presented to her readers with a gentle warmth and wry humor which adds considerably to their charm. Her descriptive abilities make an account of a fall picnic along the St. Croix more spectacular than any photograph.

It is our good fortune that her writing was not left in some dusty attic. Her words open a door to the past and give us a little glimpse of life in Nora Frye's world and her great delight in having a part of it all.

Donald G. Kelsey
B.A., University of Minnesota
Facilities Planner
University Libraries
Great-great-nephew of Nora Frye

Preface

Reading and assisting in editing the narrative essays and letters of Nora Frye has been an exhilarating literary adventure. In eminently graceful but unpretentious prose, this extraordinary woman has highlighted history, the everyday history of a "kinder, gentler" era when neighbors made Halloween dummies, endowed a librarian, and sewed abdominal bandages for hometown boys serving in the Spanish-American War.

Although she does not set out consciously to chronicle the years bracketing the turn of the century, Miss Frye has supplied readers with the ambience of those times. From the perspective of a midwestern woman with rural roots to the broader cosmopolitan view of one eventually at home in New York City and Europe, the author distills and delivers this essence by recounting selected episodes and personalities.

In addition to highlighting history, this percipient observer trains her spotlight on a fascinating array of people, ranging from rural hired men to a distinguished woman university professor. Thus illumined, these individuals become true-to-life real; they leap from print, complete with their distinctive mannerisms, peccadilloes, conversations, quirks, and virtues. And how adeptly Nora Frye underscores the lurking humor of the human condition! But while keenly penetrating, her amusement is never malicious or unkind; she does not skewer her victims.

Although few of her sketches directly involve the schoolroom, pride of profession is everywhere evident. Moreover, she writes with the trained eye and ear and pen of a pedagogue. And as she sets down her observations, she unwittingly reveals herself. Thus readers recognize her eloquent love of beauty in nature; they sense her poise in a variety of circumstances; they note the ways she embraces new experiences and ideas. A cool detachment permeates her commentary; yet her ability to form warm attachments to fellow travelers as well as family is also apparent. Her letters, especially, reveal a woman of deep affections.

Nora Frye, an amazing lady in unique times, has been nobly served by great-great-niece, Janet Panger, herself an articulate educator and traveler, who has gathered and published this captivating collection.

Virginia K. Leih, M.A., University of South Dakota
Faculty, English Department, St. Cloud State University

Acknowledgments

Iextend my sincere thanks to all who helped in any way to make this book a reality. It is not possible to mention everyone individually, but very special thanks are due to Beulah Frye Leavell, Nora Frye's niece, who kept the Frye Papers safely for so many years, provided photographs, and encouraged me to undertake the project. Thanks, also, to Miss Frye's great-nephew, John Erb, who contributed letters from her trip to Europe, and to her great-niece, Margaret Gray Hall, for the letter and photo she supplied.

For the following family members who eagerly searched their memories for details and dug through their albums to find photographs for the book, I am very grateful: Margaret Colquhoun, Daniel Frye, Mary Elizabeth Kelsey, and Elizabeth Langford.

Thanks to Marcie Shorter for the photograph of Maria Sanford's statue in the nation's Capitol, to Irene Colbenson for the photo of Rushford Normal School, and Chatfield Historical Society for the photo of the Chatifield Public School. Thanks also to Lewis and Clark High School for the photograph of the Papyrus Club and Miss Frye's retirement portrait.

Minnesota historical societies and archives have been most helpful in locating information on Miss Frye, and I especially wish to thank Rushford Historical Society, Joan Daniels, Director, Washington County Historical Society, Kurt Kragness, Executive Director, Sherburne County Historical Society, Paula Nelson, Director, Meeker County Historical Society, Fern Olson, Archivist, Carlton County Historical Society, and Alma Syvertson, Assistant Director, Fillmore County History Center, as well as the staff at the Minnesota Historical Society and Carol O'Brien, Library Assistant, University of Minnesota Archives.

Thanks are also due to Tony Greiner, Historian, Stillwater Public Library, and Raymond Fisher, Eastern Washington Genealogical Society, Spokane, Washington, Dean John F. Buenz of the Cathedral of St. John the Evangelist, Spokane, Washington, and Louis Livingston, Lois Scofield, and Louise Howard of Spokane, Washington, who shared memories of Miss Frye.

I am also grateful to the following people for their assistance: Hilda Brekke, Charles Mutschler, Assistant Archivist, University Libraries, Eastern Washington University, Zelma Pitts, Administrative Assistant, Eastern Washington University, Rebecca Kroening, Student Relations, Office of the Registrar, University of Minnesota, Richard Wassen, Coordinator, Education Student Affairs Office, University of Minnesota, and the reference librarians at St. Cloud Public Library.

In addition my thanks go to Lee Leavell, Shari Frankovic, and all of the alumni of Lewis and Clark High School, Spokane, Washington, who provided me with names of people to contact for memories of Miss Frye.

I am especially grateful to my sisters, Roberta Shorter and Marilyn Thompson, and to friends, Deborah Forstner and Beth Kiffe, who helped with proofreading the manuscript at various stages.

Very special thanks go to Virginia K. Leih for her assistance with editing and her advice and helpfulness in so many aspects of the project.

I also want to acknowledge my mother, Ann Gray Schultz, who has provided invaluable help with proofreading, titles, and suggestions for the manuscript throughout the months of preparation. And last, but not least, thanks to my husband, Ken Panger, whose patience, support, and enthusiasm have made this book possible.

Janet Schultz Panger

Contents

Introduction

This book is largely a collection of reminiscences written by Nora Frye, a native of Minnesota and a teacher who was a gifted writer, a keen and sympathetic observer of people, an adventuresome traveler, and a lover of nature.

Miss Frye's memories span her lifetime, beginning with her childhood on the family farm near Elk River, Minnesota, in the 1870s. They continue through her days at the University of Minnesota, her early years of teaching in a number of small towns in Minnesota, and conclude with her travels in Europe and experiences after retirement following forty-six years of teaching.

Told with wit and the wisdom that grows from experience, Miss Frye's stories offer the reader not only glimpses of life more than a century ago in rural Minnesota, but also of the strength and character of the author whose warmth and humanity involve the reader in a personal way.

When she retired from teaching in Spokane, Washington, in 1937, Miss Frye said she wanted to write, although not for publication. Her papers might easily have been lost had she not felt they were at least worth passing on to future generations of the Frye family. Before she died, Miss Frye gave the box containing her memoirs, mostly in manuscript form, some rewritten in several versions, to a relative for safekeeping. That relative passed them on to another relative who gave them to Beulah Frye Leavell, Nora's niece. Beulah kept Nora's papers for thirty years in her attic in California.

In 1993 I began writing to Beulah, now in her late eighties, in search of information on the Frye family. Nora's parents, Daniel and Sarah Graffam Frye, are my great-great-grandparents. I had heard that Nora had once traced Daniel Frye's grandfather, Jonathan Frye, back to his military service in the Revolutionary War, so when Beulah mentioned that she had a box of Aunt Nora's papers, I asked her to look in the box for that piece of research.

Soon after, a letter came from Beulah saying she had been unable to find the research I was looking for. However, she had discovered that Aunt Nora's papers were very interesting, and wondered if I would like to see some samples. My affirmative response prompted Beulah to send an envelope containing nine of Nora's stories with a letter suggesting that someone should write a book about her and hinting that perhaps I might like to take on that project. As I read though the packet of Nora's stories, my excitement and amazement grew; I became convinced that they would doubtless stand on their own merit and that they must be published. Thus this volume was born.

Following my trip to California in April of 1994 to visit with Beulah and other family members, Beulah's nephew, John Erb, looked though information on the family which his mother had left to him when she died, and discovered a large packet of letters Nora had written to her family during her European trip. Other relatives, all in their 70s or 80s, have also contributed photographs and additional letters to complete the portrait of this fascinating personality.

For many of us, relatives from an earlier time are known only remotely, through faded photographs and family legends. The discovery of the writings of Nora Frye has truly brought her to life for me. This book has been produced in an effort to share with others the insights and experiences of a remarkable woman whose life spanned the turn of the century and whose keen perceptions and vivid imagery allow us a rare glimpse of the past.

Janet Schultz Panger

REFLECTIONS
OF A SCHOOLMISTRESS

Nora Frye's father,
Daniel Frye, about 1898.

Nora Frye's mother, Sarah
Graffam Frye, outside the
family home, about 1910.

CHAPTER 1

The Simple Annals of Our Hired Men

Occasionally a piece of fiction of an earlier day features the hired girl, a well-known institution in rural and small-town American life. But no one seems ever to recognize the hired man, who has been largely replaced by machinery or by mass groups of workers, as the hired girl has given place to the maid. Yet some years ago on small farms the hired man was a decided necessity and more or less one of the family, whether one liked it or not.

Such a motley crowd—our hired men—mostly from northern Europe. One thing they had in common: they were all transients, though some of them stayed with us so long we felt that we had almost adopted them. When my father needed help, he had a way of picking up men at random, believing that all were honest. The remarkable thing is that for us they always proved to be so.

Often we wondered about the early lives of these men, for the manners of some of them showed decidedly good breeding. Unfortunately under the influence of drink they sometimes showed entirely different qualities. In busy seasons when harvesting and haying just couldn't wait, we used our combined efforts to keep them from town and the saloons. Happily for us, some of them were very temperate folks.

One fellow under the influence of drink surprised us greatly. That silent, gloomy foreigner who was with us for a brief time, had scarcely spoken a word until he came home one day quite drunk. "Voluble" fails to express it. He talked to anyone and everyone, whether or not he had anything to say.

He ended by staging a dramatic skit, much to the amusement of us young Fryes. As he had decided to leave us, he evidently wished to make his departure a thing to be remembered. So he went upstairs to his room, and with appropriate speeches and gestures, threw his belongings one by one out the window. He was doubtless playing to the appreciative young audience gathered outdoors below. Then with final high tragedy, he stood in the window, prepared to jump, and shouted, "Hyar I coom. To hell with it!" To the disappointment of

1

Frye family home with quarters for hired hands rear of second floor.

the young audience, however, his drama ended by his prosaic descent of the stairs on his own two feet.

A certain tall, blond German was with us only two months. As he was faithful and an excellent worker, Father hoped to keep him longer. He left us very abruptly. One day on coming hastily home from town, he dashed excitedly into the house, confided something to Father, and proceeded to pack his few belongings. It seems he had caught sight of someone he knew, and it was expedient to depart as quickly as possible. My strictly law-abiding father hurried him off with a pocket luncheon and instructions to take to the railroad track and avoid the highway.

Whatever his offense, I'm sure it was trivial and that our father knew all about it. His interest in humanity led most of the men eventually to confide in him their life histories. An hour later the local sheriff drove in and laughingly received the information that John was no longer with us.

My mind recalls another picture, and I can hear my mother remonstrating with slow, faithful Andrew. He would toss my year-old baby sister high into the air, much to her delight. To Mother's pleading—"Oh, Andrew, I'm so afraid you'll drop her," the hurt Andrew would always reply, "But Mrs. Frye, I don't intend to drop her." For he would cling with great tenacity to an idea once lodged in his mind, and he really didn't intend to drop her. Therefore he couldn't.

He seemed to specialize in mittens, having many pairs and going frequently to the house to change them. Possibly in a bitterly cold Minnesota winter he always hoped that another pair would be warmer.

The surprise of his life came to the deliberate Andrew one day when he fell off a tall load of hay. Looking up with wonder and amazement, he said, "My, but I came down fast!" Father thought he was disappointed that he hadn't time to change his mittens on the way down.

One whom we all loved and respected was a tall, dark, handsome German. He was such a perfect gentleman in every way that we were puzzled he should be in a strange country working on our little farm.

Gradually my father drew from him his story. Some scoundrel in the old country had slandered the girl he was to marry. With proper spirit John had promptly shot him and then been obliged to flee. Always he cherished lovingly the girl's picture and looked forward to the time when he could have her come to this country and marry him. Poor trusting John! How his fond hopes were dashed when he received a letter from his sister that the girl had married someone else. In bitter sorrow he burned her picture and denounced all womankind. We, too, were all highly indignant.

How disturbed we were by John's sudden unexplained departure after two years with us. He left in great distress of mind saying he had to go. As he tearfully wrung Father's hand and said goodbye to us all, he vowed that he would come back. But that was the last we ever heard of him.

Not the north of Europe or any other foreign country produced our fastidious hired man, one William Clapp. In fact he was truly one hundred percent American, born in Boston and graduated from a Boston high school. Of the scores of high school graduates I have known, never one possessed such a vast fund of information as that twenty-year-old William. He must have read widely and remembered every detail. When we came from school, perplexed by some obscure information we must find, there was William, always ready with the desired knowledge. Why he was traveling about the country, accepting a transient job on a farm, we never knew. He didn't confide in Father.

William was certainly elegant in taste and proper as to language. One evening when Father had settled down to his reading, William came in imparting the information that he had tied up the bison. "What?" said Father, not raising his eyes from his paper. When he was absorbed in the news of the day, we very well knew that his first "what" meant that he hadn't sensed what was said but merely knew that he had been addressed.

A little more emphatically William repeated, "I said I had tied up the bison."

"What, what?" asked Father, now roused from his reading.

Again said William, rather impatiently, "I have merely tied up the bison."

Pushing his glasses up on his forehead, Father exclaimed, "What in the devil are you talking about?"

Finally in despair the elegant William snapped, "Well, Mr. Frye, if you force me to say it, I have tied up the bull."

Father returned to his reading, doubtless a trifle relieved that a wild buffalo hadn't compelled him to leave the absorbing world news. And poor William settled down to meditate gloomily on the futility of trying to introduce fine language into a crude western atmosphere.

Like so many other hired men less refined, William's departure was shrouded in mystery. Temporarily disabled by an injured arm, he was not at work at the time. On some trivial errand he made a trip to town one warm afternoon and never returned. Nor did we ever find the slightest clue as to what had happened.

The young doctor who had cared for William's arm had become greatly interested in him, thinking that though there was a screw loose somewhere, the fellow after all had a remarkable mind. The doctor joined with us in dragging a pond where we thought that William might have gone for water lilies. We young people were always threatening to write a story solving the mystery of William Clapp.

My last hired man is not particularly interesting, and I should hardly remember him, were it not for a little incident about which a friend laughs to this day.

Bill was a simple, harmless American young fellow. His chief diversion seemed to be singing endless mournful songs about brave knights and beautiful ladies, foul murders and witchcraft.

Just as the early ballads were sung by people who could neither read nor write and contained stories utterly foreign to their daily lives, so our Bill evidently relieved the tedium of a humdrum life by reveling in sentimental, romantic stories.

He was clearly in the ballad stage of development, but in family affairs he was apparently not so sentimental. His stepfather in a neighboring town had died, and my brother insisted that Bill go to the funeral. Bill objected, as he was mad at his stepfather and didn't care to give him the satisfaction of appearing at his last rites. But my brother was firm and sent him anyway.

Being not much good on a farm, I was usually delegated to the easy jobs, so it fell my lot to drive Bill to town and make sure that he took the train for Anoka. I saw him safely aboard. Now it chanced that my good friend Margaret Fehr was on that same train. Remembering that Elk River was my town, she looked out, by no means expecting to see me at six o'clock in the morning. But wonder of wonders, there I was, driving a white horse down the highway and waving happily at the train. Of course she couldn't know that I was speeding Bill on his sad journey, or that he was cheerfully returning my salute. By that time he had recovered his good nature; for after all, a holiday is a holiday, even though marred by the necessity of attending a stepfather's funeral. Margaret will never get over her surprise nor allow me to forget the incident.

Potato harvest on the Frye farm, about 1916. Left to right: Deborah Frye, her father, Will Frye, and three unidentified hired men.

When I think back on our life on the farm in the seventies and eighties and the hired men who joined our family, I realize that they were not just hired men but individuals—each one with a unique personality and history. Their presence with our family certainly added welcome color and excitement to what might otherwise have been for us children a routine and predictable life.

CHAPTER 2

Letter to a Great-Nephew

June 1, 1936

Dear George,*

Your mother said you would like to know something about the family, so I'll tell you what little I know. I had to go into my trunk and get this, for I had copied it down just as Father told it to me. Remember, when I refer to Father, it is Daniel Frye, your great-grandfather.

In the seventeenth century three Fryes landed at Salem, Massachusetts with a grant of land from the King of England. Later some of these Fryes founded Fryeburg, Maine. One of them was killed by the Indians.

My father's grandfather, Jonathan Frye, was a Revolutionary War officer. Father's father was Jonathan Frye, a tanner and shoemaker who went from Maine to Nova Scotia. He was lost at sea not long before Father was born in 1823. Of course, they couldn't keep track of ships then as they do now.

Father went to a school in Nova Scotia exactly like those schools Dickens describes, with a perfectly brutal schoolmaster. But the perfectly brutal master didn't succeed in scaring the boys out of all sorts of pranks.

Father left school at an early age and drifted to Maine when he was a young man. There he visited often with an aunt of his, a Mrs. Barnes in Portland, Maine. She had the family history in manuscript and used to read it to him.

I think Jonathan Frye's people didn't think very much of the marriage he had made in Nova Scotia. Father's grandmother was one of the Lees of Virginia.

Although Father left school when he was very young, he was a great reader. He loved and read Victor Hugo and Homer all his life and could quote from memory long passages of Homer.

---

*Letter to great-nephew, George Erb.

I don't know much about my mother's people. They were American born, descended from Irish, German, and Scotch. (I think there wasn't a great deal of Irish, but as my principal insists that I'm Irish, I have to account for it some way.) Mother's home was in Corinna, Maine, a little place not far from Bangor. Father spent quite a bit of time in Old Town, Maine. He and Mother were married about 1855 and moved to Minnesota soon after. They came up the Mississippi, I imagine, as there could have been no railroads then.

Nora Frye's younger sister, Sadie, with her parents, Daniel and Sarah Frye, about 1898.

Father enlisted in the Civil War (Second Minnesota Battery) and was in it to the end, I think. He was a corporal and was wounded in the Battle of Perryville.

My mother had a pretty hard time in Minnesota while Father was away. She had the two little boys, your grandfather, and his older brother, Frank. One younger boy, just a baby a year and a half old, died while Father was away.

The Indians were troublesome, and many times Mother was frightened. A neighbor, whose husband was also in the war, and Mother used to do a good many things together. When there seemed danger of an Indian outbreak, they would drive to the fort at Anoka ten miles away.

Father lived to be eighty and Mother eighty-five.

You will marvel that an English teacher can write such a scrawl as this, but I'm in a hurry.

Hope this will help you a little.

Love to you all,

Nora

Frye family, about 1900. Back row: left to right: Silas Crockett, Ida Frye Crockett, Franklin Lee Frye, Blanche (wife of George Frye), Frank Bomberger, Clara Frye Bomberger, Nora Frye, Will Frye, Jennie Frye, George Frye. Second row Kent Frye (son of Franklin and Elizabeth), Elizabeth Staples Frye (wife of Franklin), Daniel Frye, Sarah Graffam Frye. Seated on floor: Mabel Frye (daughter of Franklin and Elizabeth), Phyllis Frye (daughter of Franklin and Elizabeth), Sadie Frye Ginder, Alice Bomberger (daughter of Frank and Clara).

CHAPTER 3

Maria Sanford: An Unforgettable Character

The memory of Maria Sanford, once known as the best-loved woman in Minnesota, has little need of my humble tribute. Not only has her biography been competently written, but her name is engraved on the hearts and minds of hundreds of college students who came under her influence.

Rather striking in appearance, by all counts she would have been a conspicuous figure, but she was doubly so from the fact that for years she was one of the two women professors at the University of Minnesota. I see her yet as she hurriedly entered her classroom, usually on the verge of being late, as she had many interests, business as well as professional. A tall, rather gaunt woman, her hair parted and drawn back smoothly into a knot, her face was plain—until her gray eyes shone with friendly interest or amusement. And when she broke into a hearty laugh, we were won completely.

Though she was always neat and immaculate, her disregard for prevailing fashions often called forth criticism. As I regard her now, rather than with the eyes of a college freshman, her ideas seem sensible. She wore her skirts short, not short according to present standards, but just short enough to give her freedom in walking and prevent her sweeping up the dust of the sidewalk. For in the nineties we wore even our street dresses long; and oh, the dust we accumulated! Miss Sanford was a busy woman and had no intention of letting clothes hamper the freedom of her movements. Also she had a passion for cleanliness. I remember once hearing her say of a society girl, "Miss Brown would scorn to take a broom and sweep a floor, but every day she sweeps up cigarette stubs and all sorts of dirt."

Rather late in life she made her first trip to Europe, as the guest of a newspaper through which she had won a voting contest. As she was preparing her wardrobe for the journey, her dressmaker protested against the short skirt. "Why, Miss Sanford, you mustn't disgrace the University, for you will really be representing it in Europe."

Nothing daunted, she retorted, "If the standing of the University of Minnesota depends on the length of my dress, it will just have to fall. I'm going to have a good time."

Her dresses were always black and severely plain. A basque [short jacket] buttoned down the front, but not so tightly as they were then worn. There had to be room for the exercise of those muscles that helped by proper breathing to produce the deep, rich tones of her speaking voice. No student of anatomy in those days would have been puzzled as to where her liver was lodged, though I'm quite sure they must have been painfully perplexed in looking at the waists of many stylish women.

Although she was actively vigorous and tirelessly energetic, I always thought of her as old, perhaps because she wore a bonnet. She was probably only in her forties when I first knew her, but a bonnet she wore with ribbons tied under her chin. She was so determined to make the most of every moment in life and waste no time that undoubtedly she felt more secure with headgear tied on firmly with no danger of a capricious wind taking it down the street and delaying her progress.

Her work at the University was teaching rhetoric and public speaking—I think we called it elocution. Happily, her public speaking was not the distressing type so common in those days, and so harrowing to the listener. Miss Sanford had the good sense to interpret a piece of literature and taught us first to understand it and then convey the meaning to our audience. So much of the work at that time was mere impersonation, with some half-baked girl trained to give a deep growl of a voice for a man—no matter what man, a mincing voice for a woman, and sort of a twitter for a child. Small wonder that it was often derisively called "yellocution."

I vividly recall a day when we were treated to that type. Miss Sanford was called away from her class, a small group reading Shakespeare. There was a visitor, a stranger to her, whom she introduced to us as a student of public speaking. She suggested that after we had given our work the young lady might consent to read for us. So when we had finished, we asked the girl to entertain us. She said that she didn't feel capable, but evidently fearing that the invitation might not be repeated, she hastily pulled off her coat and sailed in. Her choice was "The Irish Famine," and assuredly she left no horror to the imagination. Groveling on the floor she dug graves and buried the unfortunate children, the victims of said famine. Such agony! And such a voice!

The bell rang just as she finished and the class departed in haste, leaving one polite boy and me to say the proper thing to our guest, for obviously something must be said. How young we were in those days! How hard to tell even a harmless white lie in the interest of courtesy! However, the girl insisted on having our criticism. Will Morris saved the day and our reputation for truthfulness by saying most fervently, "Oh, I don't feel that we are capable of criticizing your work."

Miss Sanford taught us many things not laid down in the curriculum, things that remained with us through life. Always she stood for strength, but there was an underlying appreciation of beauty which she strove earnestly to convey to us. In the wisdom of her soul perhaps she knew that life for many of us would be hard, and she wished for us the ability to see beauty everywhere: in nature, in art, and especially in human character. Once she held up before us a great box of pansies which some student had brought her. As her face lighted up she said, "And to think, the earth might have been made without any of this beauty."

To this day when I look at a Raphael, I see the delicate grace and beauty which she pointed out. And in a Michelangelo I see the force and strength.

The beauty of her kindness reached out to many a homesick boy or girl. Though an extremely busy person, she always found time to help where she was needed. I remember her spending many hours in the hospital with a freshman boy who had been badly injured in an accident. She merely said, "He seemed to like to have me there, and he is away from home and his family."

Sometimes she was criticized for being too careful about spending money. But sooner or later one learned her history. She had come from the East when Minneapolis was booming; and carried away by the apparently great opportunities, she had bought real estate, borrowed from friends, and mortgaged to buy more. Then when the bottom fell out, she found herself greatly in debt, but not hopelessly; for she was never one to evade obligations. She worked and saved and scrimped. Years later when the debts were all paid, the habit of saving and dressing plainly had become so strong that she couldn't throw it off. We learned to accept it as part of her.

She had her eccentricities, and many odd stories were circulated about her, one of which I can vouch for, as she told it to me herself. She had once had a very serious illness, which even years later, if she became greatly overfatigued, might cause her severe intestinal trouble. She woke one cold night in the agony of cramps. Her house was a huge, old-fashioned affair with few modern conveniences. Her first impulse was to call her niece. On second thought, what a shame it seemed to rouse anyone out of a warm bed. So she went down to the kitchen, built a fire, and put on a kettle of hot water for the necessary hot foot bath.

She said she was in such misery that she could hardly lift her feet to the oven to warm them. Then as the stove heated, she began to thaw under the genial influence. And as she looked up, her lifelong passion for cleanliness overcame the physical discomfort. Surveying the walls, she thought how long it must have been since they had been cleaned. So she took the piping hot water and washed down the walls. By dawn the kitchen was clean, she had worked up a fine perspiration, and was just as well off as though she had taken the foot bath.

Years rolled by, and we forgot her eccentricities in realizing the greatness of her character. Just before World War I she retired from teaching, with a heart so damaged that she was charged by her physician to do absolutely nothing. War came on. The boys, so many of them her boys, were over there enduring terrible hardships. She must do something. All her life she had lectured. She could still go about the country lecturing and making a little money for the war effort. Who was she to be idle at such a time? Her activities led the president of the university to say that she was a woman who had retired but didn't know it. A stranger finding this white-haired woman spending the night in a day coach was moved indignantly to inquire why. To his astonishment he learned that she felt while the boys had nothing approaching comfort, she could forego a Pullman and contribute a trifle more to the cause.

So as time went on the beauty of her character and the fineness of her soul illumined her features until the face which she had always thought so very plain became really beautiful, even to strangers. In those last years of her life she was known everywhere affectionately as the best-loved woman of Minnesota.

Then came an unexpected honor. The DAR of Minneapolis asked her to go as their guest to Washington to their Easter convention.

Statue of Maria Sanford, U.S. Capitol, Washington, D.C.

She was to deliver an apostrophe to the flag, one she had written. She was an old woman who had spent her life in the service of others. But now she was the center of much loving attention. Many things were done for her. A prominent milliner, whom Miss Sanford didn't even know, requested the privilege of making her a bonnet for the occasion. Miss Sanford warned her that it must not be elaborate, as she had always dressed plainly. Happily the milliner knew how to produce an elegant creation which was at the same time very simple. Miss Sanford was greatly pleased with her bonnet, which today has a place of honor in the Minnesota Historical Society.

She was watched and guarded most carefully on that journey to Washington. When the hour came for her appearance on the program, the audience in the great hall looked at that frail, white-haired woman and settled back to rest, never dreaming that she could possibly be heard. Then to their surprise rang out that clear, strong, trained voice in her powerful "Apostrophe to the Flag." Backs stiffened in surprise, faces lighted with admiration, and there followed a great round of tempestuous applause.

That night Miss Sanford spent at the home of her old friend, Senator Nelson. After her beautiful triumph she was in excellent spirits and said it had been the happiest day of her life. Retiring early, she requested to be called for the seven o'clock breakfast with the family. Never would she wish to make extra work for maids.

Beautiful dreams must have been hers. When they went to her room in the morning, they found that she had quietly, painlessly passed away in her sleep. We who loved her were glad that she could go after such a happy day.

Maria Sanford was never a conventional teacher, but she planted in our minds and hearts a love of beauty and a sense of the dignity of human character. She taught us that all life is good, if rightly taken, and that every experience may enrich our lives if we do not let it embitter us. So I believe she was a great teacher, and I think of her in the words which Lowell once spoke of Emerson: "And after all he gave us life, which on the whole is no poor thing."

CHAPTER 4

Christie Belle

Christie Belle, that musical name with its lilting note of joy and merriment! Surely, I thought, the owner of such a name must be an altogether lovable person. Yet I knew nothing about her except that lovely name. So I was eagerly looking forward to the end of a long day's ride on the train, for Christie Belle was to meet me.

She had written from the distant town of Rushford where I was to teach in my first school, suggesting that we share a suite of rooms at a hotel: a sitting room and two bedrooms on the ground floor, all for three and a half dollars a week, with three meals a day thrown in. In answer to my hasty acceptance, she had written to say that she would meet me at the station. So as I leaned against the red plush cushions, well knowing that my freshly washed hair was full of cinders from the stove, I was not really uncomfortable. How lucky I

Nora Frye, graduate of University of Minnesota and beginning teacher, 1891.

was to be assured of companionship in a new place on the part of one generous enough to share living quarters with a stranger!

Naturally I was picturing her to myself. Christie Belle! If there was anything in a name, she would be light and frivolous. She would be young, of course, and jolly, though perhaps in a slightly restrained way; for after all, she was a teacher. Surely she would be lots of fun, and we would have good times together.

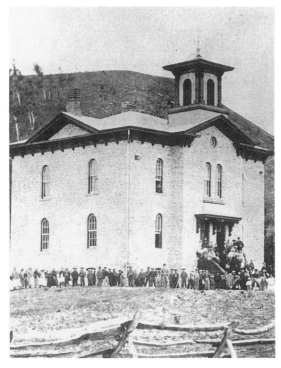

Rushford Normal School where Nora Frye first taught in 1891-1892.

At last, after stopping a long time at every little station on the way, the train arrived in Rushford, and half the town appeared to be there to meet it. I was soon to learn that meeting the train was one of the chief diversions in that little town.

Eagerly scanning the crowd, I fixed my attention on a slim, stylish young thing who seemed to be eyeing me. She had curly red hair. That surely would be like Christie. With a thrill of joy I took a step toward her; but alas! another figure loomed before me. Another not slight, not red-haired, claimed me in no uncertain terms. She was tall, heavy set, most efficient looking, and, to my disappointment, she was old. Why, she must have been at least thirty-five. And to my great amazement she wore a shawl, not a brightly-embroidered Venetian affair, but a heavy gray woolen shawl, folded cornerwise. That shawl marked the beginning of my doom.

She was pleasant enough, but her mere presence seemed to put me at once in my place. Possibly all that is meek and humble in my nature dates back to that year of living with Christie. She was so confident, so impressive, so superior in every way that I felt myself gradually shrinking as I walked by her side.

Our old-fashioned hotel was clean and highly respectable. I can still see my clothes hanging on a row of hooks at the foot of the bed in my tiny room. I was obliged to view them by the light of a kerosene lamp. A red cotton tablecloth covered our sitting room table. There was, however, one modern thing about the place. The proprietor's wife, a comfortable, plump old lady, outdistanced some of the modern flappers by smoking a pipe!

Another diversion in Rushford besides meeting the train was walking to the post office for the mail in the evening. So after supper Christie took me downtown. Even her awe-inspiring presence couldn't deprive me of a thrill of pleasure at the setting of that quaint place. I saw a little valley, shut in by high, steep hills, with two small streams running swiftly through the town. As these streams flowed into the country, great trees, drooping shrubs, and lovely flowers lined their banks.

On these trips to the post office, one was sure to meet most of the town, so Christie, wishing to start me out properly, introduced me to two bachelors whom we chanced to meet. That they were socially prominent I should have known from her very manner; but not trusting my powers of perception, she explained that they were the two most eligible young men of the town. Doing a little scouting on my own, I soon learned that their ages were forty-five and fifty. My visions of a splendid time began to fade.

Very soon I met Christie's dear friend Emma, a tall, gaunt, homely English woman. They were great card players. Often when

Emma would call for Christie to go out for an evening's game, Christie would call from her room, "Emma, are you wearing your shawl?" Now it was not the period of shawls, ancient though the time may seem. And there were so few diversions in a midwestern town in the nineties that I sometimes think those shawls saved my life.

I never knew Emma intimately. She had a forbidding air that struck terror to an ordinary soul. Recently I was interested to hear that she is still living, the fortunate possessor of a life job. The one wealthy man of the community left in his will funds for a public library with the proviso that Emma should be librarian as long as she lived. So she has the calm assurance that no change in administration can affect her. Democrats may come, Republicans may go, but her job is secure. I doubt whether even the election of Norman Thomas (Socialist Party candidate for U. S. President) would disturb her security.

When informed of her new work, did she rush off to a library school? Not Emma. She settled down calmly to manage that library in her own way. A borrower's name was entered on a certain page in a blank book; then the person was severely cautioned to remember the number of the page and line. When the borrower returned, woe unto him if he had forgotten the numbers! Knowing Emma, I fear that the ordinary business of life in the community was somewhat neglected in the mental strain of remembering numbers. All the librarian had to do was to look at the proper page, cross off the name, and then she was perfectly free. What system could be neater, more efficient, and freer from the complications of filing cards? And a life job!

Christie Belle herself was considered a person of great literary attainments. Surely she was a great reader. I have known her kerosene lamp to be burning at two o'clock in the morning, but her books were mainly the Duchess novels. You of a later generation may not be familiar with the Duchess. Her works were harmless and most satisfactory. The villain was all bad—with not a decent streak in him. The hero was handsome, bold, and virile, but morally above reproach. Often did he escape miraculously from some diabolical plot of the detestable villain. The heroine, frail and gentle, much given to weeping and swooning, never failed to marry the right man and live happily ever after. No sex stuff, no modern problems to vex the reader. What wonder that Christie burned the midnight oil!

She also had a great reputation as a teacher and was honored almost to the point of veneration by the whole community. In fact the school board never troubled to go through the formality of re-electing her to her position any more than they would have voted that the sun should rise the next day. So, great was my astonishment when the new superintendent, after visiting the little building where she and Emma held forth, confided to me that they were fifty years behind the times. And strange to say, they couldn't even keep order in their classrooms!

If I had had the proper spirit, with that knowledge and the thought of the Duchess novels, I should have held my head a trifle higher when next I walked down Main Street with Christie. But that Scotch superiority, that air of conscious virtue, always crushed me. Plainly could I detect on the faces of the natives a question as to whether I had sense enough to appreciate the advantages of companionship with a woman like Christie.

After all, there was a gentle side to her nature. A bachelor minister who came to town to hold services, to my surprise, was the object of her affectionate admiration. I see him yet, a tall, frail man, with big, mild, brown eyes—a kindly, gentle, soft nature, not well fitted to buffet the storms of life. So he was all that one would expect a sturdy character like Christie to scorn. But in serious mood, in the privacy of our own fireside, she confided to me with glowing countenance a catalogue of his virtues. I was glad to find she was human.

Effie, another teacher at our hotel, and I felt called upon to do a little matchmaking. Obviously a bachelor minister needed a wife, so we regaled him with Christie's good qualities. More and more eloquent we became as we failed to make any impression. What an economical wife she would make for a clergyman! How efficiently she would manage the Ladies' Aid! As for missions, she could make one fairly weep over the distant heathen. No one would ever dare pass up the weekly prayer meeting. Added to all this, what a literary influence she would exert among the young people. We made no mention of the Duchess novels.

Not the least impression did we make. His big, brown eyes saw no one but Effie, who was not interested in him.

After all, Christie was witty and clever in some ways. I could have enjoyed her if she hadn't directed a sharp barb of sarcasm whenever we fell into a lighter mood. She had the deadly trait of loving to hurt people.

With always two sides to a question, it is fair to ask what she thought of me. The only hint I have is that she was once heard to remark that I was "a bright little thing."

Ah! Christie Belle, of the musical name and the impressive personality, how little did either of us dream so long ago, that time and distance would embolden the crushed worm—that even after the lapse of more than half a century this "bright little thing" would dare to make you the leading character in a light, frivolous essay?

CHAPTER 5
Alice Drake
"Someday, sometime we'll understand."

These are just the words of an old song, but they bring back to me a vivid picture of one I knew long ago. The last time I saw her she was singing these simple lines in a voice that was more than clear and true, for there was some magnetic quality that drew people to her.

Vividly I can still see her, with features as flawless as though chiselled by a Greek master: rich, dark hair drawn smoothly back; great, clear, brown eyes, and perfect coloring. Her slight figure moved with calm dignity, though we knew she had suffered much.

Never before have I written of her and very seldom have I spoken of her; but since so many years have passed, I have a desire before I go hence to try to picture her. Perhaps some poetic soul will grasp my meaning and transform my crude speech into a true picture of Alice Drake, the most beautiful girl I have ever known.

I met her in her home town where I began teaching. I was young and full of ambitious dreams, still believing in the impossible. She too had started to teach, but very early in her career some sort of nervous breakdown had arrested her work. So she was living at home in a community which had no conception of her real worth.

The people talked glibly of a love affair and that she had lost her mind. Even so, she had more mind left than any of those about her. Sometimes she spoke of her illness and her regret that she could not carry a train of thought to a logical conclusion. Her conversation was interesting, even brilliant. Occasionally there would be a halt in her thought, and sadly I realized what she meant, and that her mind was not all it had once been. Sometimes there was a note of disappointment at what she had not been able to do, but never a morbid tone.

She loved teaching and had eager plans for awakening young minds to a full appreciation of the wonders of nature, the value of music, the richness of character—in a word, to full appreciation of the value of life. As I think of her now, it seems to me she had grasped all that is best in progressive education, even though she had never heard the term. What a teacher she would have made!

Many hours we spent together. Possibly she had a feeling that I was not so far as the others about her from understanding her. I have always thought of her as one so delicately constructed, so finely balanced, that it was almost impossible to go through life without some shattering tragedy. Whether it was a love affair I knew not and cared not. Certainly I never wished to know anything of her which she did not choose to tell me.

Spring came, bringing all the lush beauty of the green valley in which we lived. Together we enjoyed the beauty of trees and flowers. Sometimes we drove through leafy woods, fragrant with the wild apple blossom, the mandrake, great banks of iris and ferns, not hurrying at modern top speed, but driving a horse, which was far from unwilling to pause at every spot of unusual beauty. I always felt that Alice was more at home there than with people. We would return at night, refreshed in body and spirit.

Sometimes toward sundown we would climb one of the high hills which completely surrounded the little valley town. There, resting on beds of fragrant violets, we watched the sunset and talked of life and its meaning, and what we wanted to make of it.

On other days we followed the little swift-flowing winding river, with its flowery banks and clumps of drooping willows. As I had spent my childhood days playing on the banks of the rugged Mississippi, this always seemed to me like a play stream. I could never quite believe that it was a river.

The year came to an end and I was not to return. Leaving a reception to take a late train, I looked back for one last glimpse of Alice standing straight and fair and singing "Someday."

I see her yet, after all the long years, the beautiful oval of her perfect face, her great, soulful eyes. She was putting no outward sentiment into the words, but I who knew her heart understood what they must have meant to her. I left the room and the town with that picture in my mind.

I was young then, not used to the tragedies of life. So a little later it was a rude shock to learn that she had met her death—the hard way. But as I thought of her lovely body washed by the current into the clump of willows on the flowery bank, my thoughts were not altogether sad. For I knew that her eager, vibrant spirit must be awake on some far distant shore; and I hoped that clouds had rolled away so that at last she could understand the tragic tangle of her life on earth.

CHAPTER 6
Carrie Nation to the Rescue

A heavy step sounded through the entrance hall of the little country schoolhouse! Sudden startled looks appeared on the faces of my two oldest pupils, who saw the intruder before I did!

Then on that peaceful, balmy summer day, I turned to see a tall, haggard, desperate-looking man standing in the inner doorway. He opened the conversation abruptly: "Can you give me some liquor?"

The little school was on the main highway, but in those days traffic was not heavy. It might possibly be an hour before a traveler would pass. Unfortunately the nearest house was half a mile away. No big boys attended summer session. My ten young pupils could not be relied upon in an emergency, though my two twelve-year-old girls, with the intriguing names of Charity and Sarepta, did seem old for their years.

One thing was sure: I could count on Charity with her big, shrewd, black eyes. If I carried it off as if nothing were unusual, Charity would follow my lead and act as though a request for strong drink was just a part of the ordinary routine, a welcome interlude to break the monotony of prosaic reading, writing, and arithmetic.

Oh yes, we did also have geography. At that very moment I was teaching the boundaries of the state of Minnesota. At such a time, one thinks quickly if at all. I remembered that one must not show fear before a cross dog, a drunken man, or a maniac. Most assuredly, I was dealing with one of the two latter. And dogs! Oh, where was the dog who spent every day in front of our door? Unfortunately he had chosen that day of all days for a holiday.

Very young though I was, I succeeded in controlling my voice, which I made heavy as well as steady. Egged on by the approval in Charity's black eyes, I said calmly, "No, I have no liquor of any kind."

He looked sharply at me, as though a little doubtful, and asked if I had any medicine. He had been sick, he said, and was very much in need of liquor or some kind of medicine. Sorry to disappoint him, I replied firmly that I had nothing but water. Pleadingly he asked, "Is it cold?"

The encouragement in Charity's eyes moved me to go a step further than necessary. So instead of inviting him to take a drink from the pail in the hall, I suggested that he take the family dipper and go to the pump just outside. Through the open windows, he could easily hear me teaching the boundaries of Minnesota in my strong, schoolteacher voice.

But I had been a bit too brave, for when he had quaffed long draughts of the good, clear pump water and was returning to the hall with the dipper, there came up one of those sudden summer showers. For ten minutes it fairly poured. It was a long ten minutes, and for aught I knew the rain might keep on for an hour.

He took refuge in the hall, but I couldn't see him from where I sat. What dire plot he was contriving I knew not, but I was certain that not only was my life in danger but also the lives of the ten children entrusted to my care, a terrible responsibility. The district had provided me with a cyclone cellar but, alas, no protection against crazy tramps. The only thing to do was to teach that geography class so fiercely that even a maniac would be awed.

How bitterly I rebuked the poor innocent who gave the eastern boundary of Minnesota as New York! How sarcastic I was to the unfortunate little chap who thought the southern boundary might be Florida! Little they knew that I was fighting for their lives. But always the approval in the great, black eyes of Charity urged me on to greater lengths. Sarepta, too, was on my side; but lacking the shrewd intelligence of Charity, she hardly knew what it was all about. I couldn't keep it up forever and sometimes feared that I would collapse before the rain was over.

Charity's black eyes telegraphed that it was only a summer shower, that the man was probably harmless, and only waiting for the rain to be over. Yet there he stood silently in the hall.

At long last when Minnesota had been bounded on the west by Dakota and on the south by Iowa, the rain stopped as suddenly as it had begun. I braced myself for what would happen next. But the man, most charitably forgiving me for not keeping liquor on hand for emergencies, stepped to the inside doorway, touched his hat, thanked me politely, and was gone.

I continued teaching geography a la Carrie Nation (a militant temperance leader of the time) until he was away from the sound of my voice. Then I charged the wise Charity to watch till he was out of sight, dropped my belligerent role, and took a much-needed rest. A Carrie Nation attitude is effective but a trifle exhausting!

CHAPTER 7

Nothing Ever Happens
in a Small Town

Sinclair Lewis once wrote a unique short story—short, but with a very evident point. He first represents a young woman of literary aspirations who was bewailing the fact that she wished to write and would be able to write if only she lived where there was material. But what could she do in surroundings where nothing ever happened but the commonplace events of everyday life?

Then he cites briefly what was taking place in the lives of five different people within two blocks of the lady. In every case there was intense drama, and in some cases real tragedy.

Likewise in the placid little town of Chatfield, where I spent some years of my early life, existence was pleasant but oh, so monotonous. We were at the end of a railway stub road, and I often wondered how anything could happen in a town where the train arrived and just stayed there overnight, then went back. Nobody seemed ever to come, nobody ever to go away. When we discussed life there, I suspect we believed if we were in a city, all would be interesting. We had not lived enough to find a story in our own backyard.

Yet one day we realized that tragedy might come knocking at our very door. I had charge of the high school assembly room, and right across the hall, my friend Miss B. taught the eighth grade. One fall there enrolled in our school a tall, dark, sinister-looking boy bearing the name Ulysses Grant. No one knew anything about him, but of course we had our suspicions about the name.

He looked and acted strangely out of place at first, but very soon was accepted and liked by the other boys. This was probably largely due to the interest shown in him by Anthony Tesca, a Bohemian high school boy from the country. Dear overgrown, big-hearted, homely Anthony. I see him yet. And I respect and admire him, for he lived the religion he professed. I suspect the rest of us sometimes had our doubts about the dark boy with the unusual name. Not so Anthony. Ulysses was a stranger and a lonely one. That was all Anthony knew or cared to know.

Nora Frye, about 1897.

He took Ulysses to church and Christian Endeavor. Ulysses didn't act as though he had ever been to church before, but he accepted everything with a pleased wonder. And how he loved Anthony! Following Anthony's lead, the boys in his room at school accepted Ulysses, and he joined gladly in the activities of the school. Only occasionally there would come over him a dark mood in which he seemed to be wondering and worried. But those moods grew fewer as time went on and he became more and more involved with church and school.

One day following a revival meeting at church, Miss B. said, "Oh, you should have seen my Ulysses last night. He was at the revival meeting, and the evangelist was especially fiery, talking of repentance and forgiveness. He said that any sinner could be forgiven, even a murderer."

Happening to look across the hall, she had spied Ulysses, with glittering eyes fixed on the speaker and a terrible, tense look upon his face. "I sometimes wonder what his life has been," she concluded. "I can't forget how he looked."

Life went on much the same for months with Ulysses more and more a part of the school and Anthony growing proud of his charge.

One midwinter afternoon a sharp rap came at the door of my classroom. I opened it to see two burly men in heavy fur coats. They wasted no time in being pleasant to the lady but asked abruptly for the principal. I directed them to the office with a feeling that maybe something out of the ordinary was taking place, even in hopeless Chatfield.

School in Chatfield where Nora Frye taught in the 1890s. Photo courtesy of Chatfield Historical Society.

The rest of the afternoon was filled with little happenings, which in some unexplainable way were most disconcerting. Some time after the arrival of the visitors, the principal came to the door and beckoned Anthony Tesca from the room. After a long time Anthony returned, not at all happy or jovial, but looking crushed. When he buried his head in his arms on the desk, I was almost at the breaking point myself. But I had to go right on teaching as if nothing were happening, though quick steps and low excited voices at intervals outside my door made me sure that it was no ordinary day.

To my relief, at last four o'clock came, and the principal summoned the teachers to his office for an explanation. The two men were the sheriff of our county, and another from Kansas who had come to arrest the so-called Ulysses Grant on a charge of murder. There had been a quarrel over the boy's sister and he had killed the other man. It seems that Ulysses—I can't recall his real name—had lived in our vicinity when he was a very small child. His family was a lawless one, and the boy had never had a chance. When in trouble he had decided to go back to the place where his people had once lived. He hadn't realized that his choice of a name might arouse suspicion.

The great experience of his life came when he entered school, met Anthony Tesca, and was well treated. For the first time in his life he was associating with decent people, and no one shunned or suspected him.

He took his arrest calmly. Perhaps it was a relief to go back and face his trial. We were all saddened and deeply touched when the principal told us his history. There was another thing remarkable under the circumstances. The principal told us that the week before, Ulysses and another boy in a friendly scuffle had broken a desk. When Ulysses had tried to pay him for it, the principal hadn't been able to make the change and had put him off. But this boy being taken away on a murder charge, never to return, had remembered the debt and insisted on paying it.

Then before he left, Ulysses asked and was allowed to make a speech in his classroom. He just had to tell the other students how much he had appreciated their treatment of him and what it would always mean to him.

The Kansas sheriff had left us with the gloomy information that it would undoubtedly be first degree murder. Possibly he sensed a dullness in our town and wished to give us some excitement.

But in the course of time came the official word from Kansas that Ulysses was free. The murdered man had made a statement before his death that the boy had killed him in self-defense.

How glad we were that he had gone back to face his trial and not spent his entire life under a cloud of fear. Then came letters from him telling what life with us had done for him and that he was going far away to start again and make something of himself. His letters must have gladdened the generous heart of Anthony.

Anthony didn't finish high school, but he married a girl named Bea who was just as good and just as homely as he. They went back to the farm to live, and in the course of time, one Saturday morning I was hailed joyfully from a double wagon and was greeted by the radiant couple and proudly shown their young son wrapped in a blanket.

Now the baby looked just about as you would expect a child of theirs to look, but when I thought of the genuine kindness and nobility of those parents, I had no scruples in saying, "Why, he's a beautiful baby!"

I sometimes wonder about Anthony. Is he still living, and does he ever hear from the boy he took under his protection? I like to think that the acceptance Ulysses received in our school—the first time he had ever been received without suspicion—sent him out into the world to a useful life which he might not have had if he had not returned to that small town where he had spent his earliest years.

CHAPTER 8
Once in a Lifetime

"**B**ut I tell you I did one fool trick in my life."

I was all attention as these words were snapped out by the old lady, with an angry flash of her dark eyes. Mrs. McElderry, stiff-backed and well-preserved, seldom admitted an error in judgment. She was one of the many characters who interested me in one of the towns where I first taught. These people probably especially attracted my attention, as I had never discovered any unusual people in my own home town. There we were all very much alike: hopelessly prosaic, orthodox, Republican, one hundred percent American.

Such was not the case in Chatfield, where there was much comfortable wealth and some abject poverty, hence distinct classes of society. Plainly Mrs. McElderry didn't belong to the '400', but she had some claim to social recognition, as she had been for many years a member in good standing of the Presbyterian Church. Freely she told of the advantage of a connection with the leading church and frankly boasted of the consideration she received from the elders of the church when the obscure Mr. McElderry departed this life. She was sure those important bankers wouldn't have paid any attention to her had it not been for the church.

As she was so shrewd, so calculating, my curiosity was roused by her mention of a fool trick. Easily she was persuaded to tell her story, which like so many good ones was remote in time and place.

Her first husband, Carlyle, had died, leaving her a good-looking widow of twenty-six. According to her version, he was a stylish, dapper person, very much a lady's man. I always secretly wondered about Carlyle. Was he really a "gay blade," or was that what she wished to think after a prosaic life with the commonplace McElderry?

She lived in the South, where romance blossoms more readily than in the cold North. One day there came galloping to her door a gallant on horseback. Though he was not in armor like the knights of old, he rode a spirited horse; and from his broad-brimmed hat to his shining riding boots he had all the marks of material well-being.

Plainly he was a man of action, with no time to waste. He dismounted, doffed his hat, and bowed low. There were no flowery preliminaries, but his conversation was brief and to the point.

"Are you the Widow Carlyle?"

"I am."

"My name is Scott. I own a big plantation south of here and am pretty well fixed. Lost my wife a month ago and am looking for another. Have heard of you and want to marry you."

Thoughtfully she paused, then continued impatiently, "I was a fool. Carlyle hadn't been dead long, and I supposed I'd never marry again, so I said as much to him."

The calm self-control with which he bore the blow surely did credit to a hot-blooded Southerner. No remonstrating, no pleading, no tearing of hair!

Said he, "Do you know of any other widow around here?"

"Yes, said I, "there's the Widow Thompson just half a mile down this road. And if you get her she'll make you a good wife."

So he galloped away, found the widow, and married her.

Then she said after a little pause, "I don't know why I was such a fool! I always had a good head, and that was the only time in my life I ever did a stupid trick. He had a huge place with dozens of slaves. The Widow Thompson lived in great style all the rest of her life."

For a moment there was a dreamy, far-away look. Was she seeing herself as she might have been in ease and luxury? Then the proud old head was a high as ever, and she snapped out the words, "Yes, I did one fool trick."

With no movies, no radios, almost no shows of any kind, life in an isolated midwestern town in the nineties was not hilarious. We had to find fun where we could, so I fell asleep that night thankful for a few Mrs. McElderrys to break the monotony of existence and wondering how it would seem to have done only "one fool trick" in a lifetime.

CHAPTER 9
Predecessors

The early years of my teaching career were darkened by the shadows of my predecessors. I seemed doomed to follow those who were not only excellent teachers but who were also the embodiment of all womanly virtues. Added to that, they were all lovely Christian characters. That phrase was hurled at me so many times that it became impressed upon my memory, not to be erased in the long years that have followed.

Of all the difficulties I imagined when I went forth so bravely to my first school, the perfection of a predecessor never entered my mind. There would be problems with discipline; there might be some bravado required to teach subjects with which I was not overly familiar. I faced them all squarely in that long ride on a day train, as I leaned against the red plush upholstery, contemplated the stove in the corner, and dug cinders from my eyes.

Perhaps if I had known about my predecessor, I should not have been able to enjoy so keenly the sight of that quaint little valley town with its high surrounding hills. However, I was not to remain long in ignorance, for when I made my daily trip to the post office, I was sure to be waylaid by some interested citizen who would ask if I were the new high school teacher.

Then would follow a conversation like this:

Eyeing me closely to see that I spoke the truth, the person would ask, "How do you like our town?"

"Oh, very much. I think it is a most interesting place."

"Have you ever met your predecessor, Miss Allen?"

"No, I have not had that pleasure."

"She was a wonderful teacher."

"Yes, I'm sure of that."

"And a lovely Christian character!"

"Yes?"

Then, with a sadly critical look at me, "I don't know what the school and the town will do without her."

No more did I, so the conversation lagged. Then with a chastened spirit and a deep consciousness of my own inferiority I would go home to prepare most carefully the next day's work: eight classes, eight recitations, no two the same.

Sometimes on Saturdays I followed with delight the tiny winding river which ran through the town. It was a veritable fairy stream with overhanging willows and mossy, flower-studded banks. Forgetting my shortcomings, I returned, filled with thoughts of beauty and certain that life was good—until someone was sure to meet me with the dialogue which ran true to form.

Though in my second school I also found a perfect predecessor, my feelings were somewhat comforted by the excellence of the numerous church suppers. Ah, the good old days! We had baked hams, roast pork, great quantities of fried chicken, and salads galore, not to mention myriads of cakes and pies, all produced by those excellent old-fashioned cooks. In those bountiful days we had no food rationing, no red and blue-stamps to be reckoned with so carefully, and no scanty portions doled out. We might eat all we wished. The more we ate, the better pleased were the cooks.

Nora Frye (right) with friend, Anne Collins, and two unidentified male friends at Minnehaha Falls, St. Anthony, Minnesota, about 1897.

These bountiful meals were all for fifteen cents, though occasionally a grasping church society might charge twenty-five.

Being so well fed, I was not greatly disturbed when some well-meaning person approached me and insisted upon raving about my predecessor. Not only was she a highly-gifted teacher, but her culture seemed to have reached the whole community. It was made most impressive that the change in high school teachers had caused a letdown and produced a state of mental starvation in the town. It was hard for me to visualize any kind of starvation in the midst of such plenty.

Sometimes in my secret mind, in an attempt to maintain my self-respect, I resorted to bluff. I recalled that Oliver Wendell Holmes had written of some perfect being, whom he dubbed "the model of all the virtues." He explained that no one is ever comfortable with such people, and that they are difficult to live with. But alas! all too well I knew it was just bluff, and that mere jealousy prompted these low thoughts. Hoping for the best, I moved on to a third town, where I found many charming people, far too well-bred to remind me of my predecessor.

However, a part of the community never allowed me to forget the perfection of Miss Blake. As the Christian qualities of my predecessors seemed ever to be in the ascendant, I was hardly surprised when an ultra-pious lady assured me that Miss Blake was not content merely to gain heaven for herself, but she must take all her pupils with her. No such ambition was mine, for there were two boys in that school whom I should have been loath to accompany to heaven or any other place.

I began to despair. Was I to spend my whole life haunted by perfect predecessors? In a previous state of existence had I committed some deadly sin against them, and must I encounter them endlessly until I had paid for my crime?

But happily all things come to an end. Advanced to a larger school, I was not obliged to teach a variety of subjects, but could settle down to a program of Latin. It sounded pleasant, but I looked warily about for the familiar ghost, which somehow failed to appear. Gradually I learned the truth. My predecessor had been undoubtedly a Christian character, but she had somewhat overdone it.

An Episcopalian of an extremely high church order, she had rebuked the principal for allowing a hymn to be sung in high school. Thinking perhaps the error was due to ignorance on his part, she had explained that a hymn should be sung only in a holy place. When to her consternation he replied firmly, "Miss Bailey, this is a holy place," she had resolved to tolerate such an atmosphere no longer. So the next year there was a vacancy and a rumor that the principal in desperation looked about for the most irreligious Latin teacher in the state. At any rate, I got the job.

Miss Bailey, an excellent Latin scholar, was unable to grasp the idea that American high school youngsters are not medieval students, so she had never reached them at all. The poor bewildered pupils were relieved to find that they could learn a little Latin, while the principal, a grand old Dartmouth graduate, might indulge in an occasional hymn without fear of rebuke. I was so happy to have the ghost laid at last that I felt extremely grateful to that predecessor and earnestly hoped she would find peace in the Protestant sisterhood which she entered.

And those earlier predecessors—long ago I forgave them. After all, they were doubtless just ordinary human beings. And the years have taught me that great is the human tendency to exalt what has passed from sight. So I have no doubt that when I had gone and a modest successor took my place, I too by some marvelous transformation had become a lovely Christian character.

CHAPTER 10
Main Street: *Another View*

Sinclair Lewis with his glib pen and his merciless sarcasm has given a vivid picture of life in a small midwestern town. His *Main Street* had a great run, not alone in this country. I saw numerous copies displayed in the windows of London shops. Moreover, to my chagrin, I heard thoughtful English people comment that it seemed strange that life was so deadly in our towns outside of the cities, for in their provincial towns one found many interesting people.

In view of the fact that we had rejoiced over *Main Street*, it was vain to tell them that possibly Sinclair Lewis hadn't given the whole picture. I even go so far as to say that I know as much about small towns as he does. I was born in one and at times made my home in several others in that very midwestern state in which he lays his *Main Street*.

Furthermore, I have seen all the narrowness which an isolated section tends to produce. The amusing characters found in such a place have not gone unnoticed by me. I have laughed at small towns as much as he has, but I have never failed to find there an element of real worth, an element that does not noisily assert itself but is there to be depended upon when needed. I even go so far as to say that if Sinclair Lewis has failed to find such an element, there is something wrong with him.

With this presumptuous preamble I wish to tell you about a character I knew long ago. The very town in which he lived has furnished me subjects for more than one humorous character sketch. Yet Mr. Murphy stands out as one of the finest men I have ever known. Never did it occur to me even to wonder how he had come to be pastor of the Presbyterian Church in that little town. He and Mrs. Murphy had come from highly cultured eastern families, had traveled widely, and would have been at home in any society. But like all superior people, they were at home anywhere, and the humblest ever found in them a sympathetic and understanding friendship.

At the same time, their very superiority served unconsciously to check much that was small, gossipy, or uncharitable in the community. Doubtless they never knew how much their presence contributed to that town. I think the people there failed to realize it; but coming as a stranger, I never ceased to marvel that one family could quietly exert so much influence.

Big, blond, jovial, splendid Mr. Murphy! How we loved him! With his broad charity, keen understanding, and his ability to overlook shortcomings, he sometimes reminded me of a passage in Alfred Lord Tennyson's *Lancelot and Elaine.* Elaine looked upon the battle-scarred Lancelot and saw beneath the surface—

> As when a painter, poring on a face
> Divinely through all hindrance finds the man
> Behind it, and so paints him that his face,
> The shape and color of a mind and life,
> Lives for his children
> Ever at its best and fullest.

What a pleasant world it would be if we were always painted at our best!

While we well knew that we were only humble worms, (hadn't many preachers taken infinite pains to impress that fact upon us!) we also knew that Mr. Murphy had found in us something worthwhile.

His great charity also extended to material things. When warned that he couldn't afford to give away so much, considering that he had a family to support on a minister's meager salary, he replied that he had never seen the "seed of the righteous begging bread."* However, we sometimes felt that had not wealthy eastern friends and relatives passed on occasional generous checks to Mrs. Murphy, she might have had some difficulty in balancing the budget.

With all the love and tolerance in his nature, at the same time he was a grand fighter. I knew him in the days of "local option," I think it was called. At any rate, the community voted saloons in one year and perhaps out the next. Not even the prejudices of some rich parishioners who loved their drink could keep Mr. Murphy silent at voting time.

---

*Psalm 37:25.

One year when an unusually hot election was pending, he and his Catholic friend, Father Maddock, resolved that for one month before election they would preach nothing but temperance. And they did it with a vengeance.

Father Maddock really deserves an article all to himself. Many of his parishioners were furious, but he cared not a whit. He knew he was right, and that was sufficient for him. He even refused the big contribution which some rich saloonkeepers wished to give to the church. In no uncertain terms he informed them that he wished no blood money.

Mr. Murphy also was criticized and felt it much more keenly than did Father Maddock. One straight-laced old English lady made life wretched for him by relating to him all the adverse remarks she heard. She used to say, "Why does he preach on temperance? It offends people. Why doesn't he preach on amusements?" According to her creed, dancing and card playing would lead one straight to perdition, but she didn't feel that strong drink was a menace.

'Twas many, many years ago, but I can still see Mr. Murphy, and I'm sure that life has been richer for many of us for having known him. When I heard of his death, I wrote Mrs. Murphy, trusting that she would remember me, though I had gone out of their lives many years before. One item in her reply was of particular interest to me. When Mr. Murphy attended the fiftieth reunion of his class at Princeton, he was voted the best-loved man of the class.

While the rank and file of us had loved him devotedly, it was good to know that a group of men, some professional, others wealthy businessmen, had recognized in him the very qualities which had made him great to us.

And so when I remember Mr. Murphy and other grand souls I have known in small towns, I have the courage to say that Sinclair Lewis has given a one-sided picture. Not that what I think would make a particle of difference to him!

CHAPTER 11
Halloween Fun

It was just a little Halloween prank in bygone days. No, there was no carrying off gates or soaping windows, for we were beyond that stage. Our trick was of a different order, and it was so much fun that I always remember it at this season.

Two of us were new teachers in a very lovely, social small town. Jessie, a merry young widow, very much a society woman, had taken us to board. People just had to take us in or we must have gone home; and as we belonged to this lady's church, she took pity on us. Not only did she give us bed and board but she introduced us to the best society.

When Halloween arrived, great was her chagrin that there was no party for us to attend, probably because all the young men were off at war. No it wasn't the Revolution or the Civil War, but the short-lived Spanish-American.

After dinner she resolved that in spite of wars and the scarcity of men, we should have some sort of celebration to remember the day. So, hoping for inspiration, we all repaired to the attic. It was a New England attic with plenty of room for discarded articles and castoff finery.

Jessie's idea was to concoct a dummy that would really look like a woman. Being mere schoolteachers, we hardly thought it could be done, but we didn't know the resourcefulness of our hostess. She began with a tall floor lamp of kerosene days, with a large bulb for a head. Discreetly padded with pillows, the form was completed by a black dress. Fortunately skirts were long at that time. A black hat with a heavy veil, a fur boa about the neck, and a muff to keep the hands warm resulted in a sad-looking, respectable widow who had seen better days.

Our dummy was in no danger of collapsing, but oh, she was heavy. We were three women and a boy and figured we could carry her to the next block where some good friends lived. When she was placed before the door, we rang the bell and dropped hastily below the porch. Our trick didn't work there, owing to a very brightly-lighted hall. The lady was drawn into the house, and looking through the window we saw that our figure was causing a good deal of amusement and admiration. There was nothing to do but enter and acknowledge that the joke was on us.

But the family and their visitor all thought our prank a good one and insisted on continuing with us. This time, with two strong men to carry the lady, our progress was easy. The next place we called on was the home of Dr. Pollock, the Presbyterian minister. The dear old doctor—I can see him yet with his kind heart and his love of a joke—if perpetrated by him. He came to the door, spoke kindly to the lady and invited her in. Half turning, he repeated the invitation, "Come in," with a slight impatience. Then as he started to walk away and saw that his visitor had made no move, he said in a querulous tone, "My dear, why don't you come in?"

With wild shouts we rose from our hiding place, slightly to the discomfiture of Dr. Pollock, as he never did thoroughly appreciate a joke on himself. But he was "game," and nothing would do but he and his gentle, dignified wife must join the procession.

A few doors away was the big house of the banker, Otto Campbell. He was as jovial as any one of his grown-up children and professed himself a great lady's man. Luckily the hall was dimly lighted and there was no porch light, so our dark lady was very real indeed.

We heard a deep voice, "Good evening, come in." Then, "Come in, come in," and getting no results, he took the lady by the arm to assist her progress. At this point, confronted by his jubilantly-shouting neighbors, he laughingly said, "I didn't intend to let a woman get away."

Then the Campbell family joined us, and call after call we made upon our friends, all of whom insisted on joining us to see a neighbor get fooled. When the evening was over, there were thirty people escorting the lady in black.

The president of the school board said we had done a very fine thing, for we had furnished good Halloween fun without destroying property.

In thinking of life in that town, I recall what a writer once said, that a real society must be composed of people of all ages. We associated with those charming people of Litchfield where parents, children, and teachers all had good times together.

CHAPTER 12
Sewing for Victory

Now that peace, or what we term peace, has come, we catch our breath in relief and take a moment to look back. We have all lived through two great wars. World War I shocked us beyond measure. We hadn't realized that civilized people could be so cruel. We hadn't in our time known such a fiend as the Kaiser. But now that we have had a Hitler and his satellites, the poor old Kaiser has sunk into insignificance. Indeed he seems almost "to bear the white flower of a blameless life."

Tennyson, the faithful poet laureate, likening Prince Albert to King Arthur, once fastened this characterization upon Victoria's beloved Prince Consort. It is said that by unwittingly making him absurd, he added the last straw to the unpopularity of a foreigner who had never been received well in England. I trust that my "white flower of a blameless life" will add nothing to the unpopularity of the Kaiser, for when we consider who followed, he really seems quite a gentleman.

Some of us who have lived longer have known a third war, called the Spanish-American, which came just before the turn of the century. It surprised us, for we had been taught in school that wars must end. The ability to plant a mine and blow up a battleship must indeed show us how futile war is. As we look back, it seems a far cry indeed from the atomic bomb. But those were the "good old days" when we believed what we were taught in school.

This wasn't much of a war, but we made a great deal of it. We hadn't had a war for some time and didn't know when we should have another.

In a rather unusual way I suffered from that war. It happened just at that time that I went to a new school in a very fine town which had raised a volunteer company.

The young principal of the high school, who had the bearing and characteristics of a military leader, was sent as captain of the company. It was considered a fine patriotic thing for him to do, and he was much praised for making the sacrifice. Meanwhile, very naturally, we were expected to rejoice in the honor bestowed upon the high school, and incidentally to do his work without protest or extra pay. There being a few unruly boys in the high school, with our ensuing problems, we sometimes forgot to be glowingly patriotic. Really we were too overworked and tired to glow about anything.

But we said nothing, for pride and patriotism ran high in Litchfield. It reached the peak as Christmas drew near, and we prepared boxes for our company, which was quartered in the South.

Of course we gladly did our part, managing the high school without benefit of our principal. Still it did seem from letters sent home by our officers that they were having a very good time, the handsome captain, our one-time principal, being no exception. Letters told of most hospitable southern families, lavish entertaining, and a camp far from the scene of fighting. To be sure, that wasn't their fault, but the high school boys were very willful.

Yet we forgot our grievances as we heard of the preparations for Christmas for those older boys away from home. We hadn't much then in the way of organized groups, but women gathered in their homes, sewing machines hummed, and they willingly neglected their families for this worthy task.

Somehow they got the idea that red flannel abdominal bandages were needed by the soldiers and felt that our boys should have them. More groups gathered and more machines hummed to make two bandages for each box.

To make sure that they were doing the right thing, a delegation consulted Mr. Dickson, the stately old Englishman who had once been the Queen's banker in Calcutta. He surely would know about the needs of boys sent away to war. Very decidedly he assured them that nothing was so necessary to the well-being of a soldier as a red flannel abdominal bandage.

There were still more meetings of patriotic ladies and more humming of machines, while they made a huge box of extra bandages. No one should ever say that they weren't willing to neglect their work at home to save our boys from dysentery and malaria.

Meanwhile came more letters from officers with glowing accounts of the beauty and hospitality of southern ladies. Once the discipline of our boys at school almost drove us to the breaking point, as we had a war on our own hands at school. Then some of us were rash enough to say that it looked as though the war would soon be over, and really we failed to see what need the boys would have for red flannel bandages, considering the lively social life they were leading in the South.

Deep frowns! Charges of propaganda. Did we wish to play into the hands of Spain? They all but said we were bought by Spanish gold. We never spoke of our misgivings again.

At last all of the boxes were sent on their way, and reluctantly the women returned to their duties at home. A feeling of conscious virtue filled the air.

All would have been well if Lieutenant Campbell hadn't come home on a furlough just at that time. Of course he was besieged with questions and was kept busy delivering messages from the boys.

All unwittingly, before he knew about the avalanche of abdominal bandages that had been sent for Christmas, he gave a laughing account of the bandages that had been pouring in upon the innocent soldiers. The poor fellows were at a loss to know what to do with them. They were useful for polishing shoes and cleaning guns, but there were so many of them. In despair the soldiers had named them "Abominable Bandages."

Sadly and silently the ladies settled down to the routine of a humdrum life. After all their patriotic work—"Abominable Bandages!"

CHAPTER 13

The Doctrine of Election

Back in the quaint midwestern town of Carlton in the nineties was a character whom I could never forget. Mrs. Burton, an aged English woman, had all her life been haunted by such a fear of death and hell-fire that she had never taken any time to enjoy life.

Though I never succeeded in getting the conversation far from the prospect of her chances of salvation, I believe she was a person of no mean mental endowments. At any rate, she had produced a book of poems.

A firm believer in the Calvinist doctrine of Election (that only a few persons chosen by God in the beginning would gain heaven) she didn't dodge the issue, but lived in constant fear that she might not be one of the elect. Though believing that her fate was directed by some power entirely beyond her, she was most careful of her conduct. I'm sure she never went to a show, even the most carefully censored church performance, while to dance or play cards would have been a direct invitation to Satan. At times she was rather amusing in her prejudice against amusements. Yet liquor didn't come under the ban of her disapproval. As it was in the days of local option, feeling ran high upon the question of saloons. But Mrs. Burton was not a supporter of the temperance movement.

I wasn't much acquainted with that doctrine of Election, and it puzzled me somewhat. As salvation was beyond her control, why not indulge in a few harmless worldly amusements? Possibly she went on the principle of the woman who had her children bow their heads when the devil was mentioned. It might not do any good, but it was just as well to be on the safe side. For whatever reason, Mrs. Burton took no chances.

As she was sensitive about her age, no one knew how old she really was. She had great energy, and in true English style could easily walk the length of the town. But she looked so old and shriveled that at times she reminded me of nothing so much as Rider Haggard's *She*.

If you ever stooped to that lurid novel, you will remember that She had been young and gloriously beautiful for two thousand years or more as the result of going through a magic fire. At last, meeting the man of her choice and naturally wishing to prolong his life and youthful good looks, she piloted him to the fire on a weird jaunt up hill and down dale. Though possessed of considerable courage, as he looked at that great wall of flame, he was overcome by a perfectly natural human fear. To reassure him, She went again through the fire. But alas! the second experience undid the work of the first, and to her dismay, poor She came out looking her age.

I'm sure Mrs. Burton might better have told her age, for she couldn't possibly have been as old as she looked. Probably her terrible fear of death kept her alive for many years.

Sometimes she told stories of her youthful days in England, and one didn't have to be a student of psychology to account for her sadly-marked nature. Once as a child she had told a lie. So her older brother, with the approval of an admiring, God-fearing family, held a lighted match to her hand. This little gesture was intended to give her a slight notion of what hell-fire would be like.

Again her mother discovered her and two little companions dressed up and play acting. In shocked indignation the mother cried, "Play acting! You'll be punished, every one of you."

Nodding her head, the old lady would sadly add, "And we were, for my father died before I was grown up, Mary's people lost their money, and Emma's lover was drowned at sea." What more conclusive evidence was needed that anything in the theatrical line was a deadly sin!

Yet one can't expect too much of frail human nature, and once as a young woman in England she had strayed from the straight and narrow path, surprisingly with her mother's consent. She confessed to me that she had gone to the theater to hear Jenny Lind sing. Her mother thought that just once, simply-dressed and taking a modest seat, it might not be so very wrong. Had she worn an evening gown and sat in an expensive seat, one shudders at what might have been the dire result.

Vividly I can recall how I felt so long ago, in that isolated little town, before the days of the radio or even a respectable victrola, with some of us so hungry for music, and I listening to someone apologize for having heard the Swedish Nightingale.

She went on sadly to say that her friends thought she would be saved if anyone were, but that she herself sometimes had her doubts. Suddenly, wildly, these words came into my head: "You poor warped creature. It isn't your fault; but I too have my doubts, for I don't see how anyone so out of harmony with a beautiful universe could be happy in heaven."

That time her great age saved her. I didn't say it.

CHAPTER 14
Benefits of Church Membership

A perfect mine of interest and joy to me were some unusual characters in the little town of Carlton. Possibly in the nineties with the limited range of diversions in the Midwest we paid more attention to mere people. Yet I seldom discovered unusual characters in the small town of Elk River in which I grew up. There we seemed to be very much alike—all one hundred per cent American, orthodox, Republican, so conventional and prosaic that we almost knew what to expect when anyone opened his mouth to speak. No one was rich, no one very poor.

In Carlton there were poverty and ignorance of the kind one would expect to find only in cities. On the other hand, there was also much comfortable wealth, though the owners lived rather simply and contentedly in their old-fashioned homes. Not that they hadn't known a different life, for many of them were cultured, well-educated, widely-traveled people. There was just something in the air that seemed to make for a contentment that admitted not the slightest desire to keep up with the Joneses. Such a splendid town it was with so many fine, friendly people! Such peace and quiet and lack of hurry and flurry.

However, even in the best society in the town there were some strange people, while in the lower circles there were characters the like of whom I have never met elsewhere on land or sea.

It is not easy to place on an exact social level old Mrs. McElvain. She surely didn't belong to the socially elite in town. Yet she had some claim to recognition, as she had been for many years a member in good standing of the Presbyterian Church. She was a straight, stiff-backed, well-preserved old woman. Possibly I remember her for a certain firmness and decision she possessed which excited my admiration and even my envy. She herself was not unaware of the advantages of a connection with the leading church. Once she remonstrated with a friend of mine for not uniting with the church, although the lady gave to the cause very generously of her time and money.

49

"It ain't the same," said Mrs. McElvain. "You've got to join. Now when Mr. McElvain and I came here years ago, I looked around and got the lay of the land. I saw that the Blakes and all the folks that amounted to a hill of beans was strong Presbyterians. Pa never would have noticed. I always had to do all the brain work for the family. So I sez to Pa, 'We'll join the Presbyterian Church.'"

I never saw Mr. McElvain, but from the cut of her chin and the flashing of her dark eyes, added to a certain character resemblance to the Rock of Gibralter, I'm sure Pa joined without a protest.

When her husband died later in life, she reaped the benefits of her decision. Mr. Blake was plainly the leading citizen of the town—banker, president of the school board, elder in the church, and prominent in all good works. Though stiffly conventional and conservative, he was one of the finest men I have ever known. This comment is a bit of tardy justice on my part as I confess to then having occasional impatience with so much conservatism.

Proudly after her husband's funeral, Mrs. McElvain was wont to say, "Yes, it's a good thing to belong to the church. George Blake and the other elders come right here and made quite a fuss over us after Pa died. They wouldn't have paid any attention to us if we hadn't belonged to the church."

I wonder what would be the effect on society if we were all as frank.

Many amusing stories were told of Mrs. McElvain by people who had lived in Carlton since the early days. Mrs. Frost, with her stately duchess air and her keen sense of humor, had lived there most of her life and seemed to have a good story about everyone. One incident loses much in my repetition, but Mrs. Frost's rendition of it was as good as any modern show, for she was a born actress.

It happened one Sunday morning when a large class of young people were to unite with the church. When the minister checked over the class, Mrs. McElvain's stepdaughter, sixteen-year-old Belle, was missing. After a pause, the minister said that perhaps Mrs. McElvain could tell whether or not Belle was coming.

There came no modest response of "yes" or "no." Perhaps she had heard and always resented the idea that women should keep silent in church. At any rate she rose in her place, rocking with a swinging motion the baby in her arms, and in a clear, firm voice said, "Well, you see it was this way. We live out a piece in the country, and we got up pretty early this morning so as to get ready for church. Belle, she got ready first, an' she sez, 'I think I'll just run over to Johnson's and maybe I'll go to church with them.'"

"The Johnsons live a little ways east of us. There's several grown-up boys in the family.

"I sez to Belle, 'Now, don't you stay too long, for you've got to be on time today.' But when we was ready, she hadn't come back, so we had to come without her. I don't know where she is, but never mind. Don't wait for her. Go on with your meetin'. Belle can lay over."

She sat down. All through the speech she had been rocking the baby in her arms. This occurred in the "good old days" when babies were jiggled, not left to meditate in sad solitude on an unfeeling world.

The stately Mrs. Frost used to say that she was much younger then and had less self-control. Disgraceful though it might seem, she feared that she would be under the seat, prostrate with laughter. Her dignity had been completely upset, not only by the speech but by the puzzled expression of the very scholarly, dignified, new, young minister from the East, and by the sight of George Blake, for once in his sedate life having difficulty in controlling his facial muscles.

Belle's son was in my class in high school, a fresh-faced, golden-haired lad. I used to wonder whether his mother had ever properly come into the fold, or had taken a chance and just continued to "lay over."

CHAPTER 15
Beauty Is Truth

It's 1945, and it seems as though we have always been at war. As it approaches something that looks like a possible end, with the ever-increasing casualties, with the heartbreaking news that comes constantly to our friends and neighbors, it sometimes seems as though the horrors are more than one can bear. But we must keep our minds clear and our hearts strong to see it through to the end, that end which we all trust will finally bring about a better world.

So are we not justified in occasionally turning our thoughts from the war to scenes of sheer beauty? Perhaps by so doing we can return with renewed strength to the task of calmly meeting the hard things which are inevitable.

Recently my mind has gone back to a favorite haunt in the early years of the century. I lived in Stillwater, a small city on the Minnesota side of the St. Croix River, which forms a boundary between that state and Wisconsin. It was easy enough to take a boat and go a few miles up the river, find a choice spot by a spring of clear water, have a picnic, and drift home by moonlight.

The shores were all ours in those days, as the people seemed not to have discovered their beauty. One reason they never found our private retreat was that there were still logs in the river; and we, undaunted, had often to get out of our boat and pull it over a log jam before arriving at our destination. Now that the river is clear of logs, our favorite places have fine summer cottages and "no trespassing" signs. Incidentally, much of the beauty has also been destroyed.

I'm glad we were pioneers. We usually seemed to land on the Wisconsin side, which had higher bluffs and more rugged beauty. We picnicked at the foot of those bluffs and sometimes climbed part way up the steep hills.

In the level space at the foot were great boulders which had fallen from the heights and formed a resting place. Shaded by the dense woods, they were heavily coated with moss out of which grew delicate ferns, Dutchman's breeches, anemones, and other spring flowers. Sometimes the sides of the boulders exposed to the sun were covered with masses of pink primroses. Trillium were as common as buttercups here.

And the violets! Never have I seen such masses of them. I can never forget one large, clear, level space completely overlaid with lovely ones, most of them blue, but some yellow, some white. Once we found a bed in which the varieties had become mixed, white with blue centers. All the blossoms were large, and the stems at least six inches long. And everywhere were maidenhair ferns and other dainty varieties of foliage. On the Minnesota side we once found great masses of the yellow lady-slipper or moccasin flower, which is Minnesota's state flower.

In the fall when most of the flowers were gone, the trees with their autumn colors were a breath-taking sight. The Wisconsin side was a mass of brilliant red from the hard maples mingled with the vivid yellows to the occasional pines dotted in this riot of color. The evergreen is much more beautiful among bright colors. In the calm, late autumn weather that bluff was a gorgeous sight as we rowed away from it under the setting sun.

When we stayed until evening and silently drifted home by moonlight, how sane and healing the old earth seemed to us who loved to come into actual contact with it. I sometimes agree with Keats: "Beauty is truth, truth beauty. That is all ye know on earth and all ye need to know."

CHAPTER 16

First Aid

"Nora, are you awake?" A low, frightened voice pierced my dream, but failed to awaken me.

In my lonely little sleeping cabin, night sounds were rare, except for the occasional twittering of a bird, the scampering of a squirrel across my roof, or the rustling of the wind in the oaks.

Again came the call, a little louder, and now I was wide awake. It was two o'clock, that eerie time of night when the life stream ebbs low! My sister's voice! What dire calamity had made her dare to ascend the hill to my lonely quarters? Her cabin was close to the ranch house where my brother lived. Neither she nor my brother's wife could have been induced to brave the perils of sleeping where I did. Nor would any other perfect lady have risked the dangers of the night birds, the squirrels, and the oaks.

Hastily I unhooked the door and let her in, a pathetic figure in a long white gown. Then came her scared voice: "There's a bug in my ear. I can hear it buzzing. Will you get it out?"

As I had no light but a candle, she returned to her cabin for a lamp, giving me time to collect my wits, for I was far from feeling the calm assurance with which I had answered her. I must rally my forces. She had appealed to me. I must not fail her, but what should I do? I watched her leave her cabin carrying the lighted lamp. My time was short. The lamp was coming up the hill.

Reviewing my past life, I found no training for such a crisis. Why hadn't I been taught really vital things? Of what use was my beloved Latin in a case like this? Did my years of Greek prepare me to take bugs from ears or to do anything else, for that matter?

Anxiously I saw the lamp coming nearer. I must think rapidly. Hastily I surveyed my bare little cabin for remedies. A bottle of olive oil raised my spirits for a moment. Surely that would be harmless. But would the creature like oil and come to the surface for more, or retreat in disgust, causing greater havoc! And there was the lamp a little nearer.

My past life seemed so useless, but at last someone needed me, someone had sent a cry for help. I must not fail. I would rise to the occasion. Perhaps when I saw or heard that bug I would know how to deal with it.

The white figure and the lamp were in the room at last. Fearfully, but with a bold front, I pushed back the curly hair and peered into the ear. There was no bug in sight, not even a sound of one. It was horrible to contemplate. Perhaps it had already reached her brain. But a little bluff could do no harm. I assumed my most confident air.

"Are you sure there's a bug in your ear?"

"Well, maybe there isn't. I don't seem to hear it anymore. Perhaps it was just in my hair."

I watched the white-robed figure and the lamp go down the hill and safely enter the cabin. Then I breathed a sigh of relief and great satisfaction. In a time of danger I had shown coolness and efficiency and had covered myself with glory. For had I not successfully administered first aid to my first and only victim?

CHAPTER 17
As Others See Us

It was a hot summer, and I was spending a vacation on my brother's farm in Minnesota. Work in the fields was pressing, and help was scarce, so my offer to drive a wagonload of milk to the creamery a mile away was gratefully accepted. I was warned that it might be a long siege, for the creamery was badly managed, machinery often broke down, and sometimes there was much waiting involved before the line of customers could be served. So I hitched up the horses and took a book, preparing to enjoy myself in an emergency.

The creamery ran true to form. Something did get out of order, and as far as I could see, the men were chiefly occupied with sitting around telling yarns.

Ready for a long wait, I settled down with my book, but I wasn't allowed to enjoy it in peace, for a chatty little woman came over for a visit. As she set forth the doings of her everyday life, she proved more interesting than my book.

Leaving her breakfast dishes on the table, she had driven four miles over a rough road in a heavy lumber wagon. It would be nearly noon when she returned. There would be the hearty midday meal to prepare. After that, without afternoon rest, she would work in the fields till supper time. In the evening, she would take care of the odds and ends of housework.

As I proved to be a very sympathetic audience, she didn't stop with the work but gave me a full account of her ailments, any one of which should have barred a woman from heavy work.

I forgot my book. I forgot that I had sometimes found my work a bit hard. I forgot that I had ever been tired. My only thought was the terrible lot of that frail little woman. Oh, the injustice of a social system which would permit such a state of affairs! I talked much of it later at home, but the family couldn't figure out who the woman was.

However, the mystery was finally solved. The next Sunday when my brother returned from a trip through the woods to his hay

56

meadow, he reported that he had found my martyred woman. It was Gusty. Well, who in the world was Gusty?

She lived in a shack on a poor piece of land not far from my brother's meadow. Her husband was Charley, a shiftless, lazy fellow, not overly bright and far from easy to look at. Once when Gusty was complaining of him to my brother, he asked her why she had ever married him. She replied that she didn't want to, but her father had commanded her to take him, as she was twenty-four years old, and it was an offer. At her age there would probably never be another, and he wanted no unattached females withering on the parent stalk.

So Gusty's homely romance had ended in a life of toil. On that hot Sunday morning she was engaged in "bugging potatoes," or, to be more explicit, shaking the pests off the potato plants into a pan.

However, hard and disagreeable work hadn't taken the edge off her curiosity. She had recognized our horse from the creamery and insisted on knowing all about me from my brother.

"Is she married?"

"No, never has been."

"What does she do?"

"Teaches in a high school."

"How old is she?"

My brother protested that at this point he had hedged, but she wormed the truth out of him: I was thirty-five years old.

One more question came: "How much money does she earn?"

At the mention of the stupendous sum, Gusty for a minute stopped work in astonishment to exclaim, "My! That's a pile of money!"

Will Frye seated on the potato digger with Frye family home in background, about 1916.

Then turning vigorously to a potato plant heavily besieged by bugs, she said heartily, "But I'd rather not have it than be an old maid."

That summer my brother greatly enjoyed telling the story to my friends, and he always added, "But you couldn't really appreciate it unless you could see bow-legged Charley with his foolish grin and his corncob pipe standing idly by as he watched Gusty at her work in the hot sun."

CHAPTER 18
Are Teachers People?

Some years ago in Detroit the friend I was visiting and I were on a very small bus, where the seats extending the length of it were very close together. Just across from us were seated two women with faces about as humanly sympathetic as the ordinary meat axe. However, they looked lovingly at their young hopefuls, who were hanging dangerously off the rear of the bus. After shouting warning to the girls, one uttered this dire lament. "Poor little things! Pretty soon they'll have to go to school. I'm so sorry for them."

This noble sentiment was capped by her companion: "Isn't it awful! Those dreadful teachers. I don't see what you can expect of children when teachers are what they are!"

I was still in the profession, and my friend had been a teacher. Evidently they caught our amused expressions, for after an embarrassed silence on their part, one of them, with a sigh, made this generous concession: "Well, I suppose after all, teachers are human and have their feelings like other folks."

I was humbly satisfied to be so kindly dismissed, but my friend, always a fiery little body, said she was tempted to lean over and say, "Oh no, madam, you are entirely mistaken. Teachers don't have feelings."

CHAPTER 19
The Halfway House

" **J**ust look at the old Sheldon place. There isn't a thing left as it used to be."

I heard only this chance remark as we were driving over the Jefferson Highway (Minnesota State Highway 10) last summer in the vicinity of my old home. But it opened the door to a host of memories which came crowding in from childhood days. I looked with sad resentment at the modern stucco bungalow with its unfamiliar surroundings which had replaced the former house. Then I closed my eyes to shut out present impressions. The years rolled away and a picture of other days came clearly to my mind.

In place of the bungalow stood the old halfway house, a big frame structure, stark and bare, devoid of any architectural adornments. It was originally a hotel or stopping place, halfway between St. Paul and St. Cloud, serving to accommodate stage passengers and others traveling that distance of eighty miles. No smooth highway then, free from sand and mud, with all its hills and curves neatly obliterated. After the forty-mile drive, both passengers and horses were glad for a night's rest at the halfway house.

I do not remember it as a hotel. It was simply the quaint home of Grandpa and Grandma Sheldon, so called because they were the grandparents of many of our playmates.

In my memory I entered the house, where we children were always welcome. I smiled as I recalled the kitchen, for though all the rooms of the big house were furnished and immaculately cared for, the old couple, except in summer months, occupied only a small addition, which served as kitchen, living room and even sleeping room. As there were two small bedrooms opening off this room, I could never understand why their bed was in the corner of the kitchen, a big four-poster with curtains hanging from ceiling to floor. Yet it was a neat, cheerful room, with comfortable rocking chairs, flowering plants, and many canaries.

At this point, the thought of the birds set me off on a personal train, for Grandpa Sheldon had once presented me with a canary.

The gift wasn't welcomed with enthusiasm, as none of my family cared for feathered creatures in cages, and the ever-watchful family cat prevented Dick from roaming at will. But such a hardy bird could not fail to win our admiration. While other people complained of the short lives of their pets, he lived on and on past the normal life of his kind. He ate what was set before him, never even examining the cover of a package to see if it contained the proper amount of Vitamin B. While the birds of my friends refused to sing, he shrieked long and loud in a voice which sometimes almost put a stop to conversation in a naturally talkative family.

Once the vicious cat knocked over his cage and broke Dick's wing. He moped for two days, and then went about the business of living as usual, without benefit of surgery. He was indeed a credit to the hardy pioneer Sheldon family into which he was born.

One room in the old house was a puzzle to me: the long dining room of the hotel. There was something wrong about that room, for the floor rose like a low hill in the center and then sloped gradually down to the sides. Though I puzzled much over it, I never asked the cause. Anyway, maybe the elevation was the family skeleton, and the less said about it the better. So, like the Leaning Tower of Pisa, it remained a profound mystery, and I never knew whether it was built that way or just happened.

Grandma Sheldon was a real character. She lived to a ripe old age, and to the day of her death was a powerful influence in the neighborhood and in the lives of her children and grandchildren. Yet with all her force of character she retained decidedly old-fashioned ideas about a woman's place in the universe. Added to certain sterling native qualities was something which she had developed from living in a new country in the horse and buggy days, ten miles from the nearest doctor. Twice a year she went to town to do her shopping. Once she told me that she had planned to go on a certain day, but some business had suddenly kept Grandpa Sheldon at home. To his suggestion that she drive to town alone, she had replied scornfully, "Do you think I would go and carry that pocket book?" Though she exerted a powerful influence down through the generations of her family, I have an idea that today her great-granddaughters are quite willing to carry the purse.

Grandpa Sheldon was a slovenly, kindly, rather tiresome old man. We children all liked him, but our elders were wont to intimate that he was far inferior to Grandma. I think they even marveled that she had ever married him. But she had doubtless been handicapped by the age in which she grew up, a time when, to quote Susan B. Anthony, "an ambitious girl could only teach school or set her cap for the minister."

Probably there were neither schools nor ministers enough to go around. She seemed perfectly happy, and at any rate it was before the day when one might divorce an honest, kindly man, just because he told long-winded yarns without much point to them.

So vivid had been my daydream that when we returned from the city in the dusk of early evening, I looked instinctively for the big barn across the road, the barn which had sheltered so many weary stage horses. I longed to see the sorghum mill close by, where a patient horse traveled round and round in a circle, grinding out of the sorghum cane the sap which was later boiled in a huge vat into golden syrup.

I wanted to see the pump with the big watering trough, and Grandpa Sheldon with his old slouch hat, waiting to gossip with travelers who stopped with their thirsty horses. And best of all, Grandma Sheldon, stately and prim as ever, should be waving a neighborly welcome from the little porch.

But they were gone long, long ago; and not a vestige of their life remained, not even the little garden of old-fashioned flowers with the picket fence to keep out marauders. The newcomers might at least have left growing in the corner the little patch of sweet-smelling rosemary which I had always loved.

But alas! There was just a modern stucco bungalow, seeming by its very presence to belittle an old-fashioned past which it hadn't the soul to appreciate.

CHAPTER 20

Snapshots on Shipboard

On the *Zeeland* we saw nothing but sky and sea for eight days, a cloudless sky in a hot atmosphere with the sea as smooth as a duck pond. Once a passing ship was sighted, and again a school of porpoises claimed our notice. But there was little in the outside world to attract attention.

As the weather was perfect, the passengers for the most part spent their time on deck. Naturally we observed and lazily speculated about them. The *Zeeland* was a small one-class ship, so one came in contact with nearly everyone on board.

The young Irishman whose deck chair was next to mine mingled in the life of the ship and very obligingly kept me informed regarding most of the gossip. He it was who pointed out the very lively young Californian on his way to Paris to visit an aunt. His liveliness was enhanced by the fact that his cabin was stocked with the many brands of drink he had brought with him. As it was Prohibition time in the States, he was afraid he might not be able to purchase liquor on the ship. He needn't have feared. It was an English ship, and very often a grave-faced steward was seen hurrying by with a basket of bottles, discreetly covered, out of deference to the Americans.

I loved to watch two young girls, the twelve-year-old daughter and sixteen-year-old sister-in-law of a stately New Yorker who was on his way to Paris. His wife was very little in evidence, and when she did appear, wore the sad expression of one who hates the water and was going on this voyage only because the family was to live abroad for two years. But those two pretty girls with their lovely clothes and lovelier manners were a joy to all beholders. A warm voyage with never a bit of wind or fog enabled them to wear all their best gowns.

An English girl deserves a word. Seated next to me at table, she left nothing lacking in my education as to all the shortcomings of Americans. Having been in the States a year, she had ferreted out all our faults. Though always aware that we had many of them, I was

Nora Frye in 1923 shortly before her trip to Europe.

nevertheless aghast to find that they were so glaring. But awed into silence, I listened humbly as was proper.

The passenger whose fate I should have liked to follow was a plain old German woman. She attracted a good deal of attention as she was all alone and could speak no English. Strangely enough, not one of the passengers could speak German, but finally someone was found who could manage a little conversation with her. This was in 1923. We were all interested to learn that she had come to New York sometime before World War I. There she had lived happily with her son until his recent marriage. His wife refused to accept her and was unkind. So the proud old soul was going back alone to Germany. Everyone was friendly, and when she paced the deck, she smiled cheerfully at those who nodded to her. But as she gazed out dreamily over the sea, I used to wonder what pictures of her old home in Germany came to her mind. Little she realized the changes. Alas! What would the gallant old woman find when she arrived?

My last characters add the touch of drama (or melodrama) without which no voyage would be complete. We doubtless owed much to the handsome, blond Apollo whose wife was quite broken with grief at their parting. Small wonder that she was, for when the last farewells had been waved and the ship had put out to sea, the Apollo lost no time in casting about for an agreeable companion.

Before the day was over, he had chosen a vivid brunette who evidently had no scruples about an openly violent flirtation. At white heat it progressed until two days before landing.

Then to our surprise, he suddenly transferred his attention to a demure, pretty little blonde, a nursemaid in the retinue of an English family. He was just as open about it as he had been in the first affair, and the fiery brunette was furious at being discarded. Nor did she conceal her chagrin, but swore to have something done about it. On calmer reflection she doubtless realized there was no legal point touching such a case. As she was a wise young woman, and the voyage was nearing an end, she lost little time in using her charms upon the purser.

Several of us who were to land at Plymouth in the morning were a little disturbed that no purser appeared to release our valuables locked in the safe. The anxious delay finally elicited the information that at the ball the night before, the excitement had run so high, and so much liquor had been consumed that the purser was in no condition to appear. Doubtless the clamors of those wishing their money reached the ears of the quiet Scotch captain. At any rate he was heard to rebuke the purser who, sadder and wiser, murmured, "Never again."

I hope the brunette heard him.

CHAPTER 21
Laziness vs. Prevarication

"Take it from me, my dear, those lazy people don't lie. It requires energy to invent a good story, and they are too indolent to make the effort."

I might have discounted this rather startling statement, had it not come from the sprightly little southern lady I chanced to meet in Edinburgh. For I had learned that in her extensive travels she had become a keen observer of people. The study of art galleries and cathedrals she left to her beautiful young daughter, who seemed to be doing them as conscientiously as one does spring housecleaning.

When I learned that they were from New Orleans, I mentioned that my cabin-mate coming over on the *Zeeland* was from that city. When they asked her name, I had no idea it would mean anything to them, for she didn't seem like the sort of person they would be likely to know. But to my surprise, they seemed to know all about her because their daughter had attended boarding school with her. Then I made a confession, for it troubled me that I had somewhat misjudged the girl.

She was a strange, sloppy, indolent young woman. I don't a bit object to laziness, but she was dreadfully indifferent to everything. Of course, it was my first voyage and it was all an old experience for her. She was invariably pleasant, but my ravings over the beauty of the waves and the sunsets found no answering chord. Nor did the excellent meals tempt her. In fact, she never seemed to eat much of anything. It puzzled me how one could be so fat without eating.

In vain did I try to interest her in the lively ballroom scenes at night. She did nothing but sit in the cabin and laboriously shift her clothes from one suitcase to another. Like myself, she was a poor packer, and her wardrobe presented a sorry sight.

As a last resort, I tried to interest her in the salt-water baths afforded by the ship. One signed up for a certain time. A very formal bath steward rapped on the door and in sepulchral tones announced, "Madam, your bath is ready." Then clad chastely in bathrobe and slippers, one marched solemnly down the hall on the arm of the faithful steward and was deposited safely in the bath room. I never knew whether or not one was supposed to need extra support when clad in a bathrobe, but such was the custom. And since it was an English boat, far be it from me to defy time-honored regulations.

But to return to the bath—I raved over the advantages of it and at last persuaded my untidy cabin-mate to make the venture. I could sense her reluctance and congratulated myself that I had done a good stroke of work. But very soon she was back on my hands, the bath rudely interrupted, as she was sure she had seen a man looking through the glass roof of the bath room. The glass was at least a foot thick, but no argument could induce her to again take the risk. As we had no shower in our cabin, as far as she was concerned, baths were out for the duration.

The amusing part of it was that when I mentioned her name to the southern ladies, the daughter, who attended boarding school with her gleefully exclaimed, "Oh tell me, did she ever take a bath?"

When we had laughed over the incident, I made my confession. She had such a casual way of rambling on that I, who very seldom doubted the word of anyone, came to discount most of the things she said. As she shifted her clothes, she would say that her good clothes were all in her wardrobe trunk down in the hold. She didn't speak in a bragging tone, but rather like a child who rambles on making things up as she goes along. I didn't believe there were any good clothes or wardrobe trunk.

Her father, it seemed, was a well-known corporation lawyer of means. How could an able lawyer risk his reputation by sending abroad a daughter looking like her?

Gradually I learned that her indifference came from the fact that she didn't want to make this voyage at all, but her family had insisted upon it. She had a good reason for wishing to stay at home, for she was engaged to a very nice man and wished to go on a camping trip which included him. Having learned that I was a teacher, she seemed to think a certain standard was required in such a case. So in discussing the man, she invariably added, "You would like him. He is very refined." Skeptic that I was, I felt sure that he was a creation of her mind.

Then she told of Sally, a sister who was traveling in the Old World. She was very vague about her and wondered if Sally would meet her. It seemed as though Sally had cabled, but she wasn't sure. Of course I was so provincial that it seemed to me impossible one wouldn't be positive about a cable. But anyway she was sure I would like Sally who was very refined. I didn't want to think Sally was a myth, but I had my doubts. The days rolled by, and she continued to be just as vague, and I more and more certain that she was making everything up.

My first setback came when, just before we were to land, a very fine wardrobe trunk was sent up from the hold. But the surprise of my life came the next day when the tender came out to meet us at Plymouth, and there bounded toward us a tall, vivid, well-groomed Sally. I all but fainted. When they urged me to join them on a trip to Cornwall, I might have gone if I hadn't felt so terribly humble. I quite expected to see a grand, refined man drop miraculously from the sky.

The New Orleans lady explained that the girl's father was a prominent and very wealthy lawyer, but the mother had died, and he hadn't known how to bring up his daughters. It was a relief to confess all my doubts about the truthfulness of my cabin-mate, and my confession brought forth her shrewd remark: "Lazy people don't lie. It takes energy to invent a good story."

CHAPTER 22
A First Flight to Paris

My day began one August morning in London. Returning from a trip to the north, I had found the city rainy and chilly, a marked change from the lovely, sunny London I had left.

Obeying a sudden impulse, I decided to fly to Paris the next morning. It was in 1923, when passenger planes weren't so common. Though I had long had a desire to fly, it seemed rather foolish to pay five or ten dollars just to go up, circle around a bit, and tell your friends that you, too, had flown.

Now, I had been warned before leaving home to be sure to go on the Handley-Page British line if I flew across the channel, as that line had never had an accident.

It seemed very simple to buy a ticket at American Express, knowing that a taxi would be sent to take me to Croydon and that in Paris I should be met and taken to my hotel—all included in the price of the ticket. So I didn't even ask by what line they were sending me.

In my cab the next morning was a very friendly lady from Philadelphia. Also there was a sad-eyed man who bought a little bunch of heather to wear on his coat. (One wears heather for luck.)

The small French plane held ten passengers besides the two pilots. While it was thrilling to me, it was of course an antiquated affair compared with the luxurious, modern ship on which we had come over.

The Philadelphia lady and I were ushered into the nose part in front, which held four people and was partially partitioned off from the rest of the plane. Our fellow passengers in the little compartment were a young couple. His name was Jack, but I didn't learn hers, so I shall have to call her "the girl." They proved to be jolly and friendly, and I liked them very much. She was nervous about flying and didn't look forward to the trip with pleasure. When a yellow jacket flew in, she was much alarmed, probably one of those people to whom that creature causes deadly trouble. Jack promptly killed it—a seemingly irrelevant detail, but it appears again in the day's events.

At last we were off. Having always supposed that one went up with something of a jerk, I was agreeably surprised to find that before I realized it, we were well up in the air and sailing smoothly. As it was a clear day, I was much interested in watching the scenes below.

The English countryside, fascinating with its triangular fields wearing different shades of green and separated by hedge-rows, reminded me of an old-fashioned silk patchwork crazy quilt with irregular pieces of different colors; the hedge-rows were the silk stitches worked between the pieces.

When we had been up half an hour, the propeller on my side stopped. Evidently I was much like the old lady riding on the train for the first time. When there was a collision and all the other passengers were excitedly dashing about, she sat calmly on the floor with a mass of baggage piled about her. Asked if she were not frightened, she said in surprise, "Isn't this what they always do when they stop?"

I had a vague feeling that when the plane got warmed up, they stopped one engine, probably to keep down expenses. At any rate it was their business, not mine.

Then "the girl," who wasn't enjoying the trip as much as I, exclaimed in a startled voice, "Why are we flying so low? Heavens, we are going to land!"

With a laugh Jack said, "Well, half an hour ago that engine stopped, and the pilot turned right around. I thought I wouldn't say anything as neither of you noticed it. We are now back at Croydon."

Sure enough, there we were, and there we spent most of the day, for they didn't pick up another plane as we had expected but patched up the damaged one. We put in the day walking, gossiping, and lunching. Meeting the man with the heather, I reminded him that he had bought it for luck.

"And a lot of luck it has brought," was the gloomy reply.

Whereupon the Philadelphia lady interposed, "And that young man killed a yellow jacket. That's very bad luck. I didn't like it at all."

Not to be outdone, the man with the heather spoke with feeling, "Do you know there are thirteen people on that plane?"

To reassure him, I hastened to say, "Oh, there's a small baby."

"I know it. I counted the baby," he mournfully rejoined.

If signs meant anything, it didn't look promising for us. But at last, late in the day we were off, and our bad luck ended. I confess to a bit of relief when we were safely across the channel, for it would be hard luck to be drowned just as one were to see Paris for the first time.

One of the passengers was quite amazed that I, seemingly a civilized person, had never been in Paris before. When "the girl" kindly explained that I was from the States, I wondered how anyone could have failed to recognize my midwestern accent.

As long as it was light, I looked down with interest upon the French fields, not like the English crazy patchwork but resembling the old log-cabin quilts with different shades of green in oblong strips and no stitches between.

It was dark before we reached Paris, where we were all taken to our destinations in one large car. As I had a friend studying at the Sorbonne and living at a little hotel in the Latin Quarter, we had arranged that I go there. If she were away on her holiday and the hotel were full, I could have her room.

Entering a strange foreign city alone at night was disconcerting, and I hated to see my friends of the plane dropped off at downtown hotels while I went alone to the distant Latin Quarter. They very kindly urged me to call them up if I had any difficulty.

Then too, I began to be conscious that my very slight knowledge of French was inadequate. At any rate, when I pronounced the name of my street and my hotel, a gentleman very courteously explained to the driver where I was to go. I'm sure he felt that no French cab driver would ever find the place I mentioned.

To be sure, I had studied French in college and had later joined some classes, but I had never been a shining light. I seemed to be able to read it without much difficulty, but when it came to speaking it or having that rapid conglomeration of sounds hurled at me, it was another matter. However, I had boldly gone abroad alone, assured by travelers that I need have no fears, that in an emergency one could always find English-speaking people.

Little did I reckon with the Latin Quarter at ten o'clock at night! And little did I realize that after a long, exciting day, all the French in my mind would vanish as completely as though it had never lodged there at all.

The Latin Quarter looked strange and a little alarming in the dark, but confidently I trudged up the stairs of that dingy little hotel on the busy, noisy Boulevard Saint-Michel. When I referred to my friend, Miss Borresen, and the arrangement made for me, the proprietor firmly shook his head. My French and my frantic English could elicit nothing but sign language to the effect that he had never even heard of Miss Borresen.

The terrible thought came over me that I was in the wrong place in Paris at that time of night. But I was assured that it was the St. Louis Hotel on the Boulevard Saint-Michel. I didn't tear my hair, but I did grow somewhat excited and vehement in my protestations that they must know something about Miss Borresen. Just as firmly he shook his head with rather a startled expression, induced no doubt by the fear that he was dealing with an insane woman, and a foreigner at that. How I wished that I had gone to the Continental Hotel with the others, in spite of the price!

However, help is usually just around the corner, and in this case it appeared in the person of a young, sympathetic maid. She knew no English, but her kind heart led her to try an experiment, so she brought out a handful of letters addressed to Miss Borresen. With joyful relief I seized upon them, exclaiming in loud English, "That is she. That is my friend Miss Borresen."

Relief spread over the face of that French proprietor. "Oui, Oui, Mademoiselle Borrésen, Mademoiselle Borrésen." Doubtless he still had a notion that I was crazy, but only mildly so.

When the little maid took me to my room, I managed to convey to her the information that I was hungry. Kindly she tried to find a restaurant where English was spoken, but they were all closed at that time of night, so she took me to a very nice place near the hotel. But everything was as distinctly French as I was American.

As before, all French had left my tired, weary brain. Yet I did recall the word for a thick soup and ordered that, hoping it would contain nourishment enough to sustain me until I could muster another word. English food hadn't appealed to me, as it seemed so heavy and tasteless; but that soup was a masterpiece. I was just considering taking another order of it instead of racking my brain for the French for more solid food, when wonder of wonders, that blessed waiter, who knew no English but did know the tastes of Americans, brought me a sizzling steak with French-fried potatoes.

I have always remembered, to the credit of the French, that before that meal was over, the hotel people sent the little maid down with their card. I don't wonder that they feared I was irresponsible enough to get lost in getting back the few steps to the hotel.

Much cheered by the good food, I returned to my hotel, and by sign language I succeeded in getting a bath. The meal and the bath completely restored my drooping spirits. Then the humor of the situation began to appeal to me. Sitting in my room all by myself, I literally rocked with laughter. Here I was alone, stranded in the Latin Quarter with little knowledge of the language, to say nothing of an utterly lacking sense of direction, a trait which has always caused me to be lost, even in cities I know well.

I was to have a few days before going south to meet my friends. What might not those days hold for me! With my stupid ignorance of the language and of the customs of the country, I might even be arrested. Wild thoughts ran through my head as I sat laughing all by myself in that little French hotel. My situation would work itself out in some way. Things always did.

At the end of that jumbled day, I had the vision to feel with the "pious Aeneas," the hero of Virgil's great epic. He and his little band of followers had been pursued and buffeted by unfriendly gods until it seemed to his heartsick men that they could endure no more. Whereupon Aeneas rose majestically above his ordinarily pious, stilted remarks, to a delightfully human speech: "Courage, my men, press on. These woes will yield us yet a pleasant tale to tell."

After a good night's rest I was able to muster a little French—or what I thought was French, although I was never able to make much out of the rapid volleys of it when hurled at me. Yet I had a good time for a few days wandering about the Latin Quarter. I didn't trouble to do much sightseeing, for after a trip to the South, I was to return and spend some weeks in Paris. My sense of humor saved me from embarrassment when I would laboriously summon my French to ask the way to a certain place only to be answered by a bored voice in perfect English, "But Madam, where do you wish to go?"

Sometimes it is even an advantage not to understand the language. One pleasant, sunny afternoon I was wandering about the Luxemburg Gardens, interested in merely watching the people. On discovering that one might purchase the right to sit in a chair, I paid my coin and got a green ticket with which I might have a chair in another part of the park. But when I moved to a different section and calmly seated myself in another green chair, I was confronted by a fierce individual in the shape of one of those very disagreeable French women who are engaged as caretakers. It was evident that she felt I had no right to a chair, even when I displayed my green ticket. I felt like asserting my rights, but such a barrage of abuse assailed me that I finally moved on. She talked too fast for me to attempt to follow her, and anyway, I think my lessons in French had not included the bad names she called me. After all, I was rather glad that I couldn't understand her. Later I learned that I had committed the grave error of occupying a chair with arms when my ticket called for one without arms.

It's a strange thing to find those awful women in a country where the people are so very polite. In the lovely Paris Opera House, there they are to check your wraps, insisting upon it whether you wish them checked or not, and to usher you to your seat. I have even heard that they will refuse to show one to his seat without an adequate tip. They are probably pensioners of the government. At any rate they are not chosen for their personal charm. Lucas, the English writer, calls them "harpies" and says they would never be tolerated in England.

When I had returned from the South and was seeing Paris in a leisurely fashion, I thought that my French had somewhat improved. But the day before I left for home, I had another jolt.

I was to meet my friends at that famous little Café de la Paix, with its many outdoor tables, a place so popular that if you sit there for a little time, you are almost sure to meet someone you know.

When the waiter came for my order, I explained to him in my best French that I was waiting for friends and would order later. Immediately he departed with no puzzled look on his face, so I was sure finally my French had so improved that even a Frenchman could understand me. Such a satisfaction to feel that at last I had mastered the most difficult thing. I had labored over it, but surely it had been worthwhile.

But short-lived was my triumph, for as I looked up from my dream of satisfaction, there was my waiter approaching confidently with a tall glass of beer. I humbly drank it.

I was almost glad to be leaving the next morning. Paris was delightful, but it would be a satisfaction and a help to my pride to be where my midwestern speech with its flat vowels and rolling r's would be understood.

As I drank the beer, I pondered somewhat upon the French people. On my arrival, without a hint on my part, I had been served a dinner of delicious beefsteak. On my departure I was given beer, which I have never liked.

I thought of that old copybook saying, "The French are a gay people, fond of light wine and dancing." And I wondered if they have a maxim which their youth must learn: "Americans are a stolid people, fond of beefsteak and beer."

CHAPTER 23
Venice

I was frightened, horribly frightened. Night was coming on with almost terrifying rapidity, with only the narrow canal and the grim boatman in the end of my gondola! I saw nothing on either side but tall, forbidding stone buildings. Probably they had once been palaces, but to me they looked much more like prisons. Even so, had there been a gleam of light in any of them, they wouldn't have seemed so threatening. And this was Venice, the city of my dreams. Ironically I recalled the parting words of an old New York friend:

"Oh, but you will be simply thrilled with Venice. Get in at evening. Be booked for a hotel on the Grand Canal. Get your gondola and go sailing down, piloted by a picturesque gondolier. It's gorgeous."

Much advice had been given me as I set out alone for the Old World. Most of it I promptly forgot, but I carried always a vivid picture of Venice. Being an American, I thought of it in a blaze of light, like Broadway. I had pictured myself in that lightly moving gondola with not a trace left of the worn-out schoolteacher but a dreamy, indolent grace, varied at times with a proud and haughty air, a sort of cross between the Lady of Shalott and Cleopatra. A handsome gondolier with a scarlet sash completed my picture.

All through England and Scotland I had looked forward to Venice as a place of joy, for there would be all the light and color of the South, and there I should meet my friends from Vienna and travel no more alone.

After a lively, noisy night in Milan I was all for Italy. The afternoon ride down to Venice didn't dampen my spirits, for the Italians in my compartment, though speaking no English, were most courteous to me. I felt just a little strange in the motley crowd at the station, but an interpreter called a gondolier to take me to my hotel. At last I was in a gondola.

After a few moments I seemed to be taken entirely away from people. I had thought there would be other gondolas piloting the crowd to the Grand Canal. But not one of those people did I see in that endless ride of fifty minutes. Occasionally we did meet another gondola with its solitary gondolier. Their approach was announced by a sound somewhat between a hiss and a grunt. The canals are so narrow and dark that the gondolas would surely collide if they didn't signal when going around a corner.

It wasn't exactly what I had been led to expect. The canals seemed like the narrowest streets in the slums of New York, but much worse; for one might dodge through the crowd and run on a street, but how could one run on a canal?

We couldn't carry on an animated conversation for I knew no Italian and my gallant escort no English. It grew darker and darker, with no lights in the houses and no sound but the gentle swish of the water. I tried to remember that this was the Old World and things were different. So at first I was only a little apprehensive and addressed my gondolier, from whom the romance was fast fading. "I want to go to the Grand Hotel on the Grand Canal," I ventured at intervals. "Si, si, Grand Hotel" in assuring tones came his reply.

Still I was not convinced. Considering my knowledge of Italian, there really wasn't much point in his saying more. But I didn't like those intervals of silence in the narrow canals with the darkness and the weird stone buildings rising on either side. What was that silent Italian thinking? I began to wonder. Did he possibly consider me a rich American? Was he planning to rob and kill me? And who would be the wiser if he did? So at last I was thoroughly frightened.

Then all too late I began to think of home. Why had I ever left it? I thought of my family and my many good friends. What a fool I had been ever to find the work and confusion of the high school irksome! Come to think of it, this was September 4, the very day school would open so far away. There would be joyous greetings of friends who had been parted for the summer. They would speak of me. Little did they know I was about to be butchered by a mercenary Italian. The dark stone buildings on either side grew even grimmer.

I heard another grunt from an approaching gondola. A ray of hope came to me. Possibly this one would hold a passenger to whom I might call. Eagerly I peered into the darkness. No, my Italian was taking care that I should meet no one. The approaching craft disappeared with no sound but the swish of the water. If only they had called to each other it wouldn't have seemed so ominous.

Then I could bear no more. Quite gone were the shades of the listless Lady of Shalott; gone the vision of the haughty Cleopatra. Humped in a heap of sheer misery, I resorted to tears. Deep feminine sobs shook my wretched frame. Possibly I say it with some pride, I who have never feared the dark, nor storms, nor most things that send terror to a ladylike soul.

But after all I didn't want to die, lady or no lady, and my wrath began to rise. I would not die! Then I did some rapid thinking. Italians were doubtless craven at heart. An American schoolteacher ought to be able to put one in his place. So I rose to my full height, stepped forward, and faced that gondolier. "You are not taking me to the Grand Hotel. You know you are not taking me to the Grand Hotel." Thus I thundered in my fiercest, most commanding tones.

"Si, si, Grand Hotel," came in his most soothing tone. This time he pointed to the huge building we were approaching, which really did have a gleam of light.

My agitation had evidently prevented my seeing that we had at last entered the Grand Canal. And joy of joys! As my gondola glided softly to the veranda of the Grand Hotel, there were my friends from Vienna watching for me.

Thus ended my troubles; and sometimes so fleeting are the most vivid emotions that not later than the following morning as I awoke in that glorious city, I realized that though I had really had the fright of my life, doubtless it would someday "yield a pleasant tale to tell."

CHAPTER 24
On Our Own

1943

The terrible battles and destruction in southern Italy have carried my mind back to a happy time there twenty years ago.

1923

It was a night in Naples in a hotel close to the sea, and I had never known that so much noise could be crowded into a few hours. After breakfast on the terrace overlooking the lovely Bay of Naples, and in spite of a sleepless night, we determined on sightseeing.

As we had been in Italy long enough to learn a few things, we started out on our own. But one doesn't travel long alone in that part of the world, and three American women must need guiding and protection, no matter if they had succeeded in protecting themselves for so many years. Then too, American women who could travel about the country must be rich, even though their clothes are shabby.

Well, our American independence took us to a train headed for Pompeii, our objective for the night being Sorrento, though we had no idea how to get there. After we boarded the train, apparently we needed to decide nothing of our method of procedure, for the young man who attached himself to us would do all the planning and could take us from Pompeii directly to Sorrento for a big sum. He was so friendly, so courteous, and spoke such good English that we were almost convinced we would be missing the opportunity of a lifetime if we did not allow him to be our guide. Still we hesitated. Our follower even wanted to take care of our coats and other impedimenta while we viewed the ruins of Pompeii, but we checked them instead.

The ruins proved amazingly interesting, and the guide was so human and intelligent that we grew communicative, told him our plans, and the offer of our would-be conductor. Charging us not to quote him, he assured us that we need pay no such sum. We could simply walk down the track a quarter of a mile to New Pompeii, there get a carriage, drive to Castellamare, and take an electric train to Sorrento.

Our young man outside the walls, cheerfully waiting for us, was a trifle disappointed at our decision. Generously he had only our interests at heart, for he assured us it was a church day and there would be no cabs in New Pompeii. He didn't wish us to have our walk for nothing. We were skeptical, for when did a church day in Italy ever interfere with collecting a fee from a tourist? And not being accustomed to so much solicitous masculine attention, we were inclined to follow our own judgment. So off we started, carrying our baggage, which we had reduced to little more than toothbrushes for this hurried trip.

It was the drowsy time of a drowsy day, and the sun was dazzlingly hot. The lizards darting everywhere fascinated me, and I was half asleep, though walking. So when about halfway to New Pompeii, our would-be escort came hurrying to overtake us, I merely thought that it was a sign of his great friendliness toward us and accepted him as I did the shiny lizards. Not so Marian, the youngest of our trio. She lorded it a bit over Jessie and me because she was married and so much smarter about asserting her rights. It would seem that the necessity of looking out for oneself might develop certain qualities of independence, but Marian saw no proof of it in us.

When we neared New Pompeii and saw a whole line of empty horse cabs, Marian quickened her pace and approached a boy driver whose carriage was a little apart from the others. Still half dreaming, I didn't notice that our follower had gone over to the long line of cabs. But when we overtook Marian, who had completed her transactions with the boy, suddenly all was confusion.

To my amazement and horror, up ran a terrible-looking, bearded bandit, gesticulating wildly, cursing and shaking both fists at Marian. What in the world had Marian done! Had she, unbeknown to us, attempted to poison the Pope? It was before Mussolini's day. I was inclined to hesitate and face the music. But Marian impatiently commanded us to get right in—it was all right. So we were persuaded to try the carriage, which was so small it almost groaned under our weight. All the while our mad bandit was threatening and commanding, and our would-be guide looked sadly reproachful. What it was all about I had no conception. We were far from home and friends, and I still feared that we might land in an Italian jail, charged with heaven only knew what crime.

Our driver could speak no English, but he recognized Marian's voice of authority, whipped up his horse, and escaped. Then as I looked back upon the line of disappointed cab drivers, the truth dawned upon me. Our friend of the day had done just what Marian anticipated, urged one of them to scare the life out of the women and the boy.

Laughing heartily, we galloped through the town; then safe from pursuit, we proceeded at a leisurely pace through the country. Such satisfying glimpses of rural life we had nowhere else enjoyed in our hurried travels! One small horse with such a load couldn't possibly travel at break-neck speed. So we could view at close range the little houses of the peasants, the handsome children in colorful garb, the stout women getting supper or standing in their doorways. The swarthy men coming home from work drove oddly-matched teams, sometimes a burro beside a horse three times his size. Jingling little bells and colorful trophies decorated their collars. The big milk-white oxen came in from their work in the fields. And over all was the charm of the lovely Italian sky. I want to keep that picture to the end of my days and forget, if I can, the present nightmare.

Our boy landed us safely at Castellamare, where we took a train which went up and up over the high hills overlooking the Mediterranean, as blue as any painting can ever possibly make it.

That evening at Sorrento in our hotel high above the sea, from my balcony I looked out on a scene of rare beauty. There was the brightly-lighted, curving shore of Naples and old Vesuvius with its ever-threatening cloud of smoke. There was Sorrento with its quaint attractions, and when the sun rose, there would be the heavenly blue sea below. Italy, as always, had charm and power to stir the imagination.

Tomorrow there would be the Isle of Capri, with the mysterious Blue Grotto and that rocky coast so dangerous to sailors that the ancients thought it the home of the Sirens.

Ulysses, in his years of wanderings, had heard the Sirens, and in spite of all his hardships must have had a mighty interesting time. Under the spell of it all, I was inclined to agree with Tennyson, who makes Ulysses slightly bored and longing to set out once more from his snug island home, which he had safely reached after such great dangers.

As I looked out from my balcony that night, I found one of those rare moments when all the difficulties of life are forgotten: discomforts of travel, sickness, poverty, old age, wars and rumors of wars; and I could quite agree with Ulysses that "life piled on life were all too little."

CHAPTER 25

The Blue Grotto

"And just think! We might have had this whole day in Sorrento."

Wearily I raised my head, still dizzy from seasickness, and broke the silence which had enveloped us on that train trip from Sorrento to Naples. My companions, listless for the same reason, roused to an attitude of indifferent attention. Then Marian with spirit and a dash of malicious envy said, "Well, anyway, you saw the Blue Grotto."

It all began on the previous evening when we reached Sorrento after a strenuous, exciting day. Our hotel, the famous Vittoria, high above the sea, was most attractive; and the view from the balcony of my sleeping room was something to remember always—the curving harbor of Naples, old Vesuvius with its line of electric lights and ominous cloud of smoke. At the most, we could have only two nights and a day in Sorrento and were planning to return to Naples by boat on the second morning.

A glimpse of fascinating shops and heavenly views had made me wish to linger right there. So when I stepped out on my balcony that evening after dinner and drank in the peaceful beauty, I recalled our hurried trips from one city to another, our endless packing and unpacking of bags, and resolved to have one day of peaceful leisure. But when I communicated my intention to my companions, they said most emphatically, "Well, we are going to the Isle of Capri in the morning."

I protested a bit, in order to bring out all their reasons for going. Though I longed for rest and peace, I didn't want to miss something I should regret all the rest of my life. Bitter experience has taught me that the places I stay away from are always the most interesting. The concerts I miss are the most wonderful. The sermons from which I willfully absent myself are always the most inspiring.

So cautiously I questioned them, "Why must you go to Capri?"

"Well, it is a little island right out there in the Mediterranean."
That didn't excite me. I explained that most islands were surrounded by water of some sort.

But this, they said, was an island of special interest, the seat of many villas of the Roman Emperor Tiberius.

"But then," I retorted, "they are only ruins, and heaven knows we are all fed up on ruins. I want to contemplate the beauties of nature for a change."

Then in awed tones they produced another card. There was on Capri a cliff, still known as the Leap of Tiberius, a thousand-foot-high precipice from which the victims of the Emperor had been hurled.

I had something to say on that score. In spite of the awful reputation given Tiberius in the last years of his life on Capri, more than one authority, in the interest of justice, states that there is no foundation for these scandals except the *Annals of Tacitus*, which appeared eighty years after the death of Tiberius.

While Tacitus was a brilliant writer, the *Annals* are really not history, but historical novels. Before their appearance, no public man in Rome had a cleaner record than the old Emperor. So the critics see no reason to believe that he indulged in such cruel excesses in his old age.

As a matter of fact, I had just been reading up on the subject, but I reeled it off as glibly as though it were something I had known for years, and certainly what any well-informed person ought to know.

Sadly my friends regarded me. I was an iconoclast. I was breaking down sacred traditions. Think of all the stories that had been based on the Capri orgies!

They made me think of the pious old woman, who upon hearing some unorthodox ideas, said bitterly, "You take away my total depravity and what have I left?"

And yet I was almost sorry that I had displayed my recently-acquired knowledge. The seed of suspicion had been planted in their minds, and the Leap of Tiberius could hardly give the thrill it might otherwise have done. It's a hard world, and if one gets real pleasure out of believing that a degenerate old emperor had his victims hurled over a cliff, why disturb the illusion? But the mischief was done.

However, my friends had not yet played their trump card. They produced it at this point. Viewing me with scorn, they said they should think I would wish to see the Blue Grotto, if I had any ambition.

In our whirl of sightseeing, I had quite forgotten that famous grotto. It was known in the seventeenth century and then for many years shunned, as some superstition regarding it kept fishermen and others from entering that terrifying little opening in the side of the solid wall of rock. In the early part of the nineteenth century, it was rediscovered by a fisherman bold enough to enter. When one considers the great crowd of tourists who visit Capri chiefly to see the Blue Grotto, it seems only fair that he was pensioned for life. There followed a great wave of sentiment on the part of poets and novelists, who painted it in such glowing colors that it became one of the wonders of the modern world.

Truly the Grotto was something to be reckoned with. So the next morning, after a good night's rest and breakfast on the terrace, I announced my intention of going. My friends weren't surprised. They knew all the time I would relent.

Since the shores are too steep and rocky for a steamer to land, we were let down over the cliff in a sort of elevator to the rowboats which were to take us to the excursion boat from Naples. On that peaceful morning we learned that the lovely Bay of Naples can be a bit deceptive, for it looked innocently smooth and blue. But when we boarded that little steamer, packed with ambitious tourists headed for Capri, I noticed that most of the passengers wore looks of sad weariness and were somewhat pallid in color, varied with tints of green or yellow.

Sighting a couple with whom I had traveled through Switzerland, I learned that the Bay was rough and that from violent tossing of the boat, many people had been ill all the way from Naples. And how that boat did rock and toss! Not caring to have the day completely spoiled, I sought a bench where I lay flat with my eyes closed. My friends were sure I was seasick and thought it a great joke.

When we reached the other side of the island, the steamer stopped and we were told to get our boats for the Blue Grotto. Coming to life, I found that Marian and Jessie were too far gone even to think of changing boats. Then I looked for the entrance to the Grotto. We were faced by a solid perpendicular wall of rock, against which the waves were furiously dashing. No wonder the ancients considered it the home of the Sirens who lured sailors to ruin with their beautiful songs.

Looking for something which might be an entrance to the Grotto, I discovered a very small semi-circular opening, not more than three feet high. In wonder I exclaimed, "Do we have to go through that little place?"

I was told that it was the only entrance to the Grotto. Many row-boats circled about our steamer. They are of necessity small, and only two passengers besides the boatman are allowed.

I hesitated. The waves were so high, the wall of rock so forbid-ding, that entrance so dreadfully small, that the whole adventure looked almost too perilous. Still I hesitated. Maybe the Grotto wasn't worth it. A spirit of cowardice made me prefer to be with friends if I were to be dashed to pieces. Just then Mrs. Lutz, my chance travel-ing companion in Switzerland, came to the rescue. I couldn't under-stand what possessed her, for being a splendid sport, she never wanted to miss anything. Furthermore, she had been looking for-ward eagerly to the Grotto. But she looked at the sea, she looked at those little boats, she looked at that tiny opening in the wall over which the waves were dashing. Then she said firmly, "I'm not going. You and Mr. Lutz go together."

She was heard to remark about its being an awfully small open-ing and she was a big woman. As her husband and I were both on the thin order, she evidently thought we could go through safely. Mr. Lutz wasn't a lifelong friend, but he had been a pleasant traveling companion, so I had better go ahead and die with him if need be.

Our steamer was still rocking when we made the change to the little rowboat, which gallantly rode those high waves. It was a relief to experience a different motion.

As we neared the opening to the Grotto, I willingly obeyed the order to lie down, for I didn't care to have my head broken on the rocks. There was considerable fuss on the part of the boatman, much shouting, and fierce grasping of a cable fastened to the rocks. Then we were within the cave. After the roaring, dashing sea, it was a place of pure delight.

Walls, roof, water—all are an exquisite blue. Someone has said that the water does not seem like water, but rather like folds of shimmering blue satin moving around and beneath in luminous, transparent waves. The hand dipped in the water gleams like silver. Indeed it is an amazingly beautiful place; but in spite of the beauty the boatmen do not linger long, for if the sea becomes too violent, an exit is impossible. On rare occasions travelers have been detained there for twenty-four hours.

I noticed that our boatmen were gradually edging toward the opening, over which the waves were dashing higher and higher. A little appalled, I saw the boat just ahead of us strike violently against the wall of rock at the side of the opening. It might have been done for effect, but I didn't like it. So when our turn came to lie down in the boat, I pulled my hat over my eyes. I didn't want to see what happened. Even Mr. Lutz admitted he was frightened.

But after a few minutes I raised my head to find we were again in the open sea with many rowboats surrounding us. With shouts of triumph, the boatmen welcomed us as though we had been saved from a burning building—then tried to sell us strings of coral.

Here it was that my troubles really began, for the excitement in addition to the return to that unholy motion of the sea played such havoc that I became desperately ill.

When we reached the steamer, I found my friends more or less recovered but complaining that the rocking of the boat when moored was worse than when actually moving. It seemed to them that we had been gone for an age. Somehow they conveyed the impression that it was my fault, but I was past caring.

Back on the other side of the island, we were taken to the hotel at the top of the cliff for luncheon and then to see the ruins. Marian, the inveterate shopper, said she would have luncheon and then look up the shops. Horrors! Luncheon! I wanted never again even to hear of food.

Fortunately in the deserted reception room of the hotel there were two couches. Jessie and I dropped down upon them and spent in exhausted sleep our chance of a lifetime to see the ruins of the villas of Tiberius. But I had feverish dreams about the past.

With a mind poisoned by the scandals, I saw the wicked old Emperor with his harem of lovely young girls swimming in the Grotto. How their silvery bodies gleamed! Gossip says that after sporting about in the water, he strangled them. Then I saw him dancing in mad glee as his tortured victims were thrown over the thousand-foot leap. Down, down, down endlessly they went.

Just then my dream was broken by a faint voice from the other side of the room, "Don't you think we had better order some tea?" It was the last thing on earth I desired, but it seemed only fair to pay something for our lodging.

A silent trio, we went back to Sorrento, from which some hasty planning enabled us to return to Naples that night by train. Not one of us could bear even to think of a boat trip the next morning. Subdued and gloomy we sat there, until I broke the silence by suggesting that we might have spent the whole day in Sorrento.

When I think how much my friends had counted on the Blue Grotto and how long they had looked forward to seeing it, while I had planned on it not at all, I rather think Marian was justified in a bit of malice when she retorted, "Well, anyway, you saw the Blue Grotto." And I didn't have the courage to ask if she had really seen the Leap of Tiberius.

CHAPTER 26

1937-1938
A Year in the Slums

I was to have a whole winter in New York City! Such a grand prospect to follow my retirement from forty-six years of teaching.

Always I had loved New York in my brief summer visits of a week or a month and longed to be there through the season of opera and theaters—difficult to manage on a small income. So I hailed with delight the offer of an old friend to live for a year as a boarder in the settlement house of which she was the head.

I knew very little about such places except that a group of people lived in a slum neighborhood and acted as good neighbors in the community. In return for my board, which was very reasonable, I did a little work to help out. As a matter of fact, I put in a good many hours, but I felt it only fair.

It was not a large house, but it fairly hummed with activities from morning till late at night. Seven of us besides the cook lived at the settlement, while other workers came in for the day or evening.

I was given such tasks as could be safely trusted to an untrained worker. One of my duties was to take the roll for one hundred undernourished children who came in for lunch. Little did I realize the difficulties before me: a hundred children who never enunciated clearly and never sounded the letter "r," while I had much midwestern respect for that letter.

I looked at them in dismay, and they looked back in impatient despair as they crowded about to have their names checked. Nothing in my previous experience had taught me that Chaw Claw was Charley Clark, and to them Chaw Claw couldn't possibly have any other meaning. Luckily an intelligent fourteen-year-old girl who could talk came to my rescue and acted as interpreter for a few days until I understood the language.

Another task which I found most exciting was making neighborhood calls. To the other workers it was an old story, and they were tired of it. But I loved it, and coming into close quarters with these people was a real experience for me. Always I had a legitimate excuse: looking up some child who had enrolled at the House and had not lately appeared.

More often there was a deeper reason for the call. Perhaps the settlement people had heard that a family was to be turned out by the landlord and wished to learn the truth. Or they desired to know something of the home conditions. The approach must always be carefully made, allowing none of the condescension of social workers of an earlier time.

I remember long ago hearing a society girl from Chicago discuss her slum work. As it was all new to us, we asked if it was not difficult to approach perfectly strange people. Glibly she replied that it was all very easy, as you were given a card with a list of questions which you asked in proper order.

Little as I then knew about slum people, I had visions of Question No. 1. "Is your husband at work?" Question No. 2. "Does he drink?" And I had great sympathy for the woman who once answered, "No, does yours?" Well, it's quite different now, and if one cannot make a call in the spirit of a good neighbor, she had better stay away.

It was always with a feeling of adventure that I entered a tumbledown tenement with dark narrow halls and rickety stairs. It was just alarming enough to be exciting. I must have looked properly helpless, for usually some stalwart young man acquainted with the place would offer to take me to the apartment I wanted.

Their doors were always locked, probably in anticipation of a call from the landlord for the usually unpaid rent. My escort would knock and call loudly that there was a lady waiting. Slowly, reluctantly, the door was unlocked, and as my cavalier deserted me, I half expected to be thrown down the stairs. But always people were polite and grateful when they learned I was from Goddard House. They knew I was a friend.

I remember with pleasure an English woman, Mrs. Marshall. In fact, we came to be good friends. She suffered greatly from arthritis and with increasing lameness was unable to walk to the Settlement. Some organization gave us a large shipment of bananas once a week. She was very fond of them, so I offered to take bananas to her on Wednesdays. Then I found it pleasant to stay for a little visit.

Crippled though she was, her apartment was immaculate, and she herself was always neatly dressed. Though I think she was often hungry, she would never ask for food. One day she told me she had been extravagant and given a neighbor girl a dime to get her a piece of lamb for stew. And oh, how good it had tasted with her vegetables! After that I always took her a little meat when I called. I sometimes wonder if Mrs. Marshall is still getting her bananas. I fear with the shortage of help no one has time to take them to her.

One morning about eleven I made a memorable call on the mother of ten children. I think she was still in bed, for she was summoned by her brother who was industriously scrubbing the kitchen. Such a vision she was as she appeared in a gray robe: a tall, well-proportioned, handsome woman with fine color which was not artificial. She was friendly and kindly, but I couldn't help feeling her superiority as she smiled down at me and patted me on the shoulder with a sort of "my dear child" air.

When I asked about her nine-year-old little Mary and suggested that as she was so thin and pale I wondered if she was eating properly, the mother threw up her hands in mock despair and said that Mary would just live on tea. And there you were. What could one do if a nine-year-old insisted on a diet of tea? The lady didn't appear to be drunk, though they told me at the House that she usually was in that state.

I withdrew, feeling keenly the terrible injustice of life. Faced by this magnificent creature, here I was, plain, underweight, with no color except the drugstore type. Yet I had lived a temperate life all my days. Still with all her grandeur, she had her troubles.

One of the helpers at Goddard House met her one day on the street shouting wildly for the police. While she had been attending her sister's funeral, her husband, sadly in need of money for drink, had pawned just about everything in the house including the sheets and the children's clothes. She was calling frantically upon the law to do something about it.

I was saddened by one call I made. I was to look up a family who, it was reported, were about to be turned out of their apartment, as they quarreled so terribly. As usual, I was supposed to look up the small boy who had not appeared at the Settlement for some days. I wanted, if possible, to get into their quarters, but no one at the House had ever succeeded in gaining entrance. The man of the house heard me ask for their apartment, and as he gave me the information I needed, I had no excuse to go further.

The little boy had been hurt in an accident. No, not badly. Yes, they were comfortably situated there, were staying on, and all was well. There was something pathetic about him. Polite and respectful, but not cringing. He surely had seen better days.

As we were talking, his little girl joined us, and he gently reproved her because her hair was untidy. It will be a long time before I forget that frail little girl and her wistful question, "Is there any chance to get piano lessons at Goddard House?" What heritage of a respectable ancestry was stirring in her blood! I longed to gather all the ambitious little ones, take them bodily out of the slums, and give them a chance.

At last there was no excuse for prolonging the interview, and I turned to go. The man, taking polite leave of me, went the other way. When he had turned a corner, I went back and looked up the manager. It was true that he was turning them out the next day. He hated to do it, but they were way behind with the rent. Always they promised that when the relief money came in they would pay; but always they spent it for drink. Then they quarreled so terribly that they disturbed everyone. He thought the man would be rather a decent sort if it weren't for the woman. I wonder what became of the little waif whose dream was to play the piano.

We live and learn. Gradually I began to see why so many social workers become either hard-boiled or sentimental. I am quite sure I should never be a marked success as a slum worker. My sympathies were all with the people, but I was somewhat like the well-meaning volunteer worker who offered to direct children's plays. In her contact with the not overly-clean children, the young lady wore gloves during their games. Noticing this, an artless little tot asked, "Why do you keep your gloves on? Have you got the itch?" In dealing with them at close range, I fear I should keep on gloves, literally and figuratively. And with gloves on one could never really be a success.

Yet I came away from that year feeling that the experience had been very worthwhile. Sometimes I wish that everyone might spend a year in the slums in order to realize the rich blessing of merely being born and reared in decent surroundings.

CHAPTER 27

A Hillside of Flowers

Never shall I forget my first sight of a California poppy field. Driving south from Berkeley, I had caught glimpses of beauty in the flowers growing close to the railroad track. There would be a patch of deep orange poppies, then a mass of yellow flowers. Frequently there were beds of blue lupine, and a low magenta blossom. Then two colors would be artistically combined. Finally, to my joy, on a knoll close to the track all these colors and others were mingled in a Persian carpet.

These hurried glimpses were like much of my experience in California. I seemed to be always whisked past things, while someone with a sweeping gesture would command my admiration but drive right on. Californians seemed to feel that it was enough for one to know that the beauty was there and hurry on to more. Knowing there were other beautiful spots beyond, they seldom seemed to understand that one might wish to pause and drink in the beauty of flowers and trees.

It was a clear, bright April day when we started early for the Mohave Desert. I had warned my friends that if we found flowers I wished to sit right down by them and stay as long as I pleased. When at some distance from the highway we saw vast hillsides of brilliant orange, we took the road that led to them.

Such a sight! There were several acres of the largest California poppies I have ever seen. It was one of those perfect desert days when the sun casts wonderful lights and shadows upon sky and mountains and sand dunes and flowers.

My friends sat cheerfully for hours in the sun and ate their lunch in the sand by the roadside. Though poppy fields were not new to them, they quite enjoyed my enthusiasm and probably had visions of selling me to some chamber of commerce to promote tourism.

There was a little trail down the slope through the center of the field. Finding that the poppies were seen at the best advantage from that path, again and again I walked over it. Always that desert sun made different pictures of the field. As the last one was always the most beautiful, I couldn't bear to miss any of them.

At a little distance one saw only the orange glow, but a closer view revealed much white lupine, having dainty crystal-like petals, with a tiny streak of green over the little globes. A low blue lupine helped to complete the color scheme. Bits of grass and an occasional spear of grain mingled with the mass of bright color, just enough to enhance its beauty. The green had a bluish tinge, as though one were seeing it through colored glass. The low foliage of the poppies had turned a dull red, a veritable burgundy shade.

Always I found new beauties by walking over that path and sometimes pausing long at a certain point with an olive grove in the background, low fields in front, the Sierras in the distance, and over all the beautiful desert sky.

That gorgeous field! More than ever before I grasped Wordsworth's thought that nature has power to affect the lives of people who will yield to its influence. Vividly came back to me his lines upon the daffodils:

> I gazed and gazed—but little thought
> What wealth to me the show had brought.
> For oft, when on my couch I lie,
> In vacant or in pensive mood,
> They flash upon that inward eye
> Which is the bliss of solitude.

The poppies were not dancing as did Wordsworth's swaying daffodils, for no breeze was stirring in the desert on that memorable day. But I'm sure that the flowers have brought "wealth to me," for a great joy fills my soul when I recall the picture of that flower-covered hill in its setting of desert color.

CHAPTER 28
Impressions

Hurried glimpses of beauty in the landscape were mine as the train whizzed by! As I don't like either to go to bed or get up on a train, always whenever possible I take the Great Northern day train to Seattle. My friends scorn it, preferring to retire peacefully at night, rise early, and miss all that long day of sitting on the train with nothing to do. They miss something else, but I can't convince them.

Last summer at the end of June when I made the trip, I was surprised at the wealth of beauty in the wild flowers just outside Spokane. For miles and miles there were great beds of lupine of a heavenly blue. Masses of white flowers relieved the blue, then yellow, so golden in the June morning sun. There were other colors, and occasionally they all mingled in a Persian carpet effect; and always there was the background of fresh, lovely green. Beyond them, growing out of the rocks and cliffs, were sprays of syringa and the feathery spirea. As we neared the desert, the growth changed, but always there was beauty in the mere desert colors and the strange rock formations. I think everyone enjoys the scenery when we reach the mountains with their sparkling waterfalls and a picture at every turn, but I wouldn't miss even the desert.

Then came a long weekend in a log cabin near the foot of Mount Rainier about 3,000 feet above sea level. We were right in the dense woods, with majestic trees of spruce, fir and cedar, some of them nearly two hundred feet tall, together with all the wonderful undergrowth that goes with such a forest, and many strange flowers that I had never before seen.

The huge cabin was a masterpiece, built patiently and painstakingly by the owner and his sons. Pieces of wood had been fashioned into quaint articles of furniture, rendered so beautiful that one felt that those who carved had loved the wood and brought out the best qualities it could show.

But best of all, in front of the cabin a mountain torrent roared over the rocks and cliffs. As I listened to it and watched it by the hour, I recalled the musings of that delightful naturalist, Donald Culross Peattie, for he never could get over the wonder that the cascade was always the same, and yet the crystal particles were ever changing. I also realized how he felt as he said that when he found a waterfall within sound of his window, no matter where he was, he knew that he had come home, that if any man wished to see him, he must come there to find him. And if he had nothing more important to say than the cascade, let him keep silent. Ah, the memories we have and the dreams we dream when we lose ourselves in the sound of a waterfall!

My mind shifts to a home in Montana on a high point overlooking Flathead Lake. It was just a Sunday evening party with a very jovial crowd mostly concerned with eating and drinking. I tried to be polite, but I was so absorbed in the setting that the lively human beings interested me very little. The host himself was a striking figure, a stately elderly man in white, busily cooking hamburgers on the outdoor fireplace. I envied him his rugged strength and his tawny complexion, probably brought with him from his native New Zealand.

The grounds afforded a wonderful view of Flathead Lake with its islands and inlets and high mountains beyond. There was a gorgeous sunset, frequent on that lake. We faced the west, which was a mass of flame, ever changing slowly and gradually, with high mountains everywhere and that riot of color which I shall never forget.

Turning around, I looked toward the east where the mountains of the Mission Range loomed forbiddingly near. They were not touched by the crimson sunset but had a violet shade all their own. Dark and dignified, they seemed almost to rebuke the western colors as being too gaudy to be seemly. Slowly night rose from the ground, creeping gradually over the violet and changing it to darkness.

And I thought, with all that is discouraging in this sick world today, there is still the beauty of nature which gives a promise of real peace in the world at last.

CHAPTER 29

My Journal

F or future generations who may chance to read this document, I
wish to explain that it is written under protest. I can't write a
journal, but when a charming but firm chairman of the Creative
Writing section said, "You are each to keep a journal. Begin tomorrow," I recognized the voice of authority. All my life I worked under
a system and learned to obey orders. So when the command was is-
sued, I had an awful feeling that I should have to write a journal,
though there is nothing in my smooth, idle life to write about.

Friday, October 9. I once heard a teacher of creative writing
stoutly affirm, "If you can't find material for a story in your own
backyard, you'll never find it anywhere." Living in an apartment
and having no backyard, I am slightly handicapped, but perhaps the
kitchen will do.

In my life the highlight of Friday is the cleaning woman. Strong,
cheerful, fresh-faced, she is really an attractive person. When I think
of all the things she does to make so many families comfortable, I
feel a tremendous respect for her. To be sure, she unconsciously
makes me feel like a worm, for I can't help comparing her life with
mine. However, it doesn't seem to have any visible effect upon me.

I gasp with wonder when she tells me that she went home after
her day's work, canned nineteen quarts of tomatoes out of her own
garden, and did the family ironing, then was up at six o'clock the
next morning for another day's cleaning. But though I am filled with
admiration, do I rise at dawn the next morning and sweep the floors
of my establishment? I do not. I think of all the years when my
alarm brought me to attention at 6:30 and thank heaven that I can
sleep as long as I please.

October 10. If I should say that I was once a brisk walker, I
should remind myself of the fat, middle-aged women who proudly
declare that they tipped the scales at 101 when they were married.
Just the same, I even once outwalked a charming English girl who
was visiting in this country. Dear girl! She was so delighted with our
American freedom, so pleased with everything, and so tolerant of our

Nora Frye, about 1940.

shortcomings! It was a delight to walk races with her. My hiking days are over, but there are always compensations, and perhaps I shall see more beauty in things close at hand.

Even if there isn't a story in my backyard, there is beauty just across the street. I discovered it this morning while I sat in the sunshine on a convenient bench. From my viewpoint, the house, high above the street, is almost hidden by the trees. In the foreground stands a lovely evergreen with fresh branches reaching to the ground and just back of it a maple with leaves of most gorgeous red, and then a dainty, cut-leaf birch of brilliant yellow. High above them all grows a tall, slender pine, not so beautiful as the other trees, but seeming to glory in the height it has attained. In the dense shrubbery bordering the grounds are blended yellow, red, and dull purplish hues, a fitting frame for the picture. Buses and traffic I mind not. The beauty of the scene dominates all.

October 11. On reading over yesterday's notes, I find them even more stupid than when I wrote them. But the mention of a walk with an English girl set me off on a train of thought about a walk with another English girl of a very different type. It was years later. I met her on the boat going over. She had been in this country a year, and the voyage wasn't long enough for her to tell me all our faults, so she looked me up in London. She had evidently spent that whole year searching out the weak spots in our armor. She found me an easy mark, for I refrained even from mentioning the Fourth of July. At the end of a busy day in London, we took the bus to Richmond, and finding no way to reach Kew Gardens but to walk, we walked. It was many years after my first English girl, and I wasn't so good a walker, but I would have died rather than confess it to her. Kew Gardens were worth the effort, and when we came to a patch of Oregon grape I gave a cry of delight, forgetting for the moment that no good thing could come out of this country. But when I said that it grew in profusion in the state of Washington, she skeptically leaned over, read off a long technical name, and said it came from China. But I protested, "Just the same, it's Oregon Grape, and it grows in the United States."

Examining it more carefully for signs that I was wrong, she said, "This has some blue berries on it."

"Yes," I replied, "I have made jelly of them."

She subsided. For a moment the Stars and Stripes had triumphed.

How different she was from so many English people I chanced to meet who were always so courteous, so ready to help a stranger.

October 12. I've had a visit from our niece with her four-month-old son, a blue-eyed vision of pink and white. I did not voice my thoughts, but I did wonder if twenty years from now he would have to follow in the footsteps of today's young men. Heaven grant that they may crush the tribal instinct which has risen in the world and that out of their great sacrifice may come a better world.

My favorite walk is through the evergreens on Eighth Avenue, past the hospital and the Porter place. As I lean over the fence and gaze to my heart's content at the lovely garden, I am reminded of Van Dyke's essay, "Who Owns the Mountains," in which he declares that the beautiful place or painting in reality belongs to the person who can best appreciate it. Probably if a haughty caretaker orders me away I shall reply, "Why, I own this garden."

October 13. Across the street in the hospital grounds there is a tree with the most brilliant red leaves. How brave it is! Though the leaves are soon to die, they put on their boldest colors. Perhaps in the wisdom of nature they know that death is nothing to be dreaded.

October 16. Last night our book club met. As it is unknown except to the ten women who are members, I think it deserves a bit of notice. Over twenty years ago two of us organized it, merely to get easily in touch with the latest publications. Much to our surprise, it has continued to live and flourish, for no one ever wishes to miss our monthly meeting. We purposely chose people who didn't see each other too often—some teachers, some other ladies. We buy books and pass them on. No one has ever prepared a paper or given a book review. No one ever will. Sometimes we discuss books, sometimes the affairs of the day. Sometimes we just gossip.

Last night one member, the only one who had heard Ilka Chase at the Early Bird Club, amused us with an account of her talk. Of course we had all read in the morning paper that her speech was "like a five cent cigar," what we all needed. In spite of the glowing account, some of us had our doubts, and were not surprised to hear that a good deal of it was rather cheap sophistication, probably designed to shock the women of this provincial place—and to please the men. I was mean enough to be glad that the men looked bored.

October 18. Today I received from a friend in Santa Barbara a clipping about the naturalist Donald Culross Peattie, and an article which he had written for the *New York Times Magazine* about

Cabrillo, the first white man to visit California. Mr. Peattie is very loyal to California, which he has discovered. When asked by eastern friends if he doesn't feel "terribly far away and out of things," his serene answer is "far away from what better place, and out of what?"

I think he writes most exquisite poetic prose and has done a great work in interpreting the world of nature to the rest of us.

October 20. We are all greatly distressed at the thought of younger boys being called into service. Of course the cry goes up that they make the best soldiers, but it seems so pitiful. Today I felt a little comfort in reading the following in Elizabeth Goudge's book, *The Castle on the Hill.*

> When the lethargy of their fathers allows the ramparts to crumble, the young men fill the breach. "And ye dear youth who lightly in the hour of fury put on England's glory as a common coat." Lightly, always lightly. If their banner was that of a young man dying on a cross, it was brightly colored, and it streamed in the wind. It was the old who met these times of crisis with such heaviness. The young were wiser. They sang as they fought.

October 21. Let me close with a frivolous note. A friend who has recently given up voluntarily a strenuous position—in order to show how far she has fallen from her early traditions and the classic in literature, quotes the following, which she found on a bookmark:

> If your nose is close to the grindstone rough
> And you hold it down there long enough,
> In time you'll say there's no such thing
> As brooks that babble and birds that sing.
> These three will all your world compose,
> Just you, the stone, and your darned old nose.

Letters

December 8

Dear Beulah,—

Do you mind if I answer your note with a Christmas letter? Rather early, but it will escape the rush.

I want to wish you all a very happy Christmas, and a New Year that will bring you the new house. You are wise to start all over again and build just what you want. That seems to be the way one ever gets enough room.

You surely do a lot of things, taking care of your family, social stunts.

Letter in Nora Frye's hand.

CHAPTER 30
Letters from Europe

On Board *S.S. Zeeland*
Red Star Line
Thursday, July 19, 1923

Dear family,

First I'll tell you I'm having a perfectly heavenly time. Jessie Brewer and Florence Hall came down to the boat with me and waited to see me off. Florence brought me a corsage of sweet peas to wear because she said in the movies voyagers always wore flowers when they sailed.

I had made up my mind that my stateroom would probably be a smelly little place and was dreading to enter it, so I was happily surprised to find it roomy and very well equipped—made for four people, and there are just two of us. May is from New Orleans and we are getting along well together.

There is a closet in which to hang clothes, and we really aren't cramped at all. Last night was warm and I suggested we fasten the door open a little if she weren't afraid. So we did that, and there was a grand breeze blowing through our window all night.

When I sought out the deck steward and asked for a chair, he asked, "Have you got your mail? You have about a hundred letters." The girls fairly howled when we went for it, for there surely was a fine bunch of mail, and I'm reading the letters a few at a time. Haven't finished them all yet. It will be fun to be reading greetings from my relatives and friends all along the way. I picked out the letters from my relatives to read first, and it was splendid to hear from you all. Besides the letters, there's a package in my trunk that I haven't yet opened.

It is the middle of the forenoon, and we were just interrupted by the serving of chicken broth. In the afternoon they serve tea. Yesterday we had perfectly delicious white fruitcake with it. The meals are good. Had a fine breakfast of grapefruit, broiled finnan haddie [haddock], bacon, rolls, and marmalade.

We are seated at table. Next to me is a girl who seems to have lived most of her life in England and Scotland. She tells me that I must visit the head of the police in every place at which I stop or I'll be fined $500 and imprisoned six months. So if I happen to stop off for two hours to look at a cathedral and forget to look up the police, I may stay over here longer than I intend.

I'll write a little every day. I'm having just a grand time and am enjoying every moment of it. Of course, I have to admit that the sea has been calm ever since we left. I'll probably be telling a different story before we are through.

Friday

There was a dance last night. It was a pretty sight. The crew curtained off a part of the deck and hung all kinds of flags and strings of lights. I watched the young people for a time and then retired early as I wanted to enjoy a long day today. The night was hot, and even a sheet was too much covering.

Half an hour before breakfast a man goes around beating on a brass pan. I was up before breakfast. The sun was bright and the track of it on the waves was a soul-satisfying picture.

I'm wearing my Canton crepe and no wrap, but it's not uncomfortably hot. Nobody's sick yet, but everyone says, "You wait!" However, I propose to enjoy life while I can.

Wore my gray skirt, my new blouse Clara made for me, and my gray stockings and black suede shoes down to dinner last night. There are nice people on the boat, and they are friendly without being too familiar.

By the way, the deck steward lied about my letters. I counted them last night. There are only thirty-six, plus a post card and a telegram from Annie Blitz who is to be Dean of Women at the University of Minnesota. I just finished reading the last of them this morning. I still have a number in my trunk that I shall read at intervals. It certainly was good to have greetings from all the family—two letters from Clara, letters from Sadie, Blanche, Bernice, Beulah, Elizabeth, Dorothy, and Georgia. I won't mention all the friends who wrote, but Clara, you tell Mamie that I was much pleased to find a letter from her. Sadie, you tell Mrs. Evans I enjoyed her letter and will try to look up her mother in London.

I received some presents too. Carrie and Mary Hitchcock sent me a lovely silk shirt. The book club sent me a Baedeker of Central Italy. Oh yes, Mrs. Ferguson sent me a handkerchief. When I opened the envelope that Margaret Fehr gave me at Coeur d'Alene, there was a five dollar bill and a note that I am to buy something for myself. Isn't that nice? The world is so beautiful and the people so good that I'm getting more like Pollyanna all the time. If this ship goes down, don't mourn for me, for I shall be happy till the very end and probably also happy in the next world.

The deck steward just went by, saw me writing, and said, "You'll have lots to do answering all those letters."

Instead of going straight to London, I may stay a few days in southern England. The country of Cornwall sounds interesting, and I think I might just as well see it. I hear there are some people on the boat who are going there. I am hoping to meet them and learn their plans. We will probably get into Plymouth Thursday evening. In that case I will spend the night there and start out the next morning.

This is a terribly stupid letter, but at least it will serve to let you know that I am well and happy and grateful for all you have done for me.

Friday continued

I've been resting and looking at sky and sea, and I just want to say that I shall be happier all my life for having had these three days, even if all of Europe is a disappointment. Of course, this feeling may change at any time, for I suppose we are bound to have some rough weather.

I am even too lazy to read, so don't expect me to write a good letter. Goodbye until the next time.

P.S. There are four or five jolly young fellows on board and a lot of pretty girls; so they have some good times, and it's fun to watch them. One of the bunch is a young Irishman whose deck chair is next to mine. Of course he spends most of his time with the younger folks, but occasionally he takes a rest. One very merry fellow stopped and spoke to him, and I asked who he was. He is a wealthy Californian. I said, "He seems to be having a good time." The Irishman said "He has enough liquor stored away to keep him happy for a long time." Apparently there is a lot of liquor on board, but they keep it out of sight in deference to the "drys." He said he was in a crowd last night that would have all been under the table if a few of them hadn't had sense enough to break up the party and go to bed.

Saturday morning

We've just had breakfast. Again a lovely sea. It's a little fresher, but still warm. Had a very hot night, but I rested well. I thought no one had been sick, but a girl said this morning that she had been ill all night.

I was interrupted here by word that a boat was sighted, so I hustled along to see it. It was about half an hour before we met it, and it proved to be a freight boat. A girl took me way up high, and the captain came out and talked with us. Then a young man appeared and asked if he might have permission to go to the higher point; they call it the "bridge." The captain said that was one place where passengers weren't allowed, but after a pause he said, "Well, suppose we all go up." He took us up, showed us the compasses and all sorts of other instruments, showed us how they signal other ships when they don't want to bother with the wireless. He explained the chart of our voyage and everything. The reason we stay so far south is to avoid the chance of encountering icebergs.

It's still hot, and we're still in the Gulf Stream. We shall be out of it tomorrow, but you know me well enough to know that I haven't suffered with the heat. Yesterday morning they checked the temperature of the water and found it was over one hundred degrees.

There are nice people on board, and gradually I'm getting acquainted with them. To tell the truth, I'm so happy doing nothing that the people don't interest me so very much right now. I think I shall close for the present. Clara, I wish you and Frank were here with me.

Sunday a.m.

Last night I felt very strange and went to bed early, but I'm all right this morning. I surely was afraid last night that I was in for it.

Everyone complains of the heat, but it is cooler today, and we have just seen a very beautiful sailing vessel.

Episcopal services were held in the library this morning. The Catholics are to have services in the card room, and I saw a notice that there would be eleven o'clock services in the dining room. You won't catch me going to any service down there. It's too stuffy. I've gone down for every meal so far, though.

We still have a very calm sea. Decided last night I had been eating too much, so went back to a simple breakfast after I had gone to eight o'clock service. Then walked a mile on deck and feel now that I have a right to rest.

The water temperature is lower, so we are doubtless getting out of the Gulf Stream. We traveled 413 miles Friday.

Monday morning

I just had breakfast and so continue this chronicle.

I felt bum yesterday, but found I was all right if I kept perfectly still. So I ate my luncheon on deck and lay there quietly till night. I wasn't seasick but felt strange. I think I have been eating too much, so I've cut out a lot of things and am better.

There are curtains at the stateroom doors, so we sleep with our door open and get good circulation. The ship doctor says he has never seen such a calm voyage. Clara, you tell Mr. Ellis that I'm not sick yet.

My roommate doesn't seem to be very happy. Poor thing, I feel sorry for her, but she is an awful bore, so I don't bother much with her. She is fleshy and dieting—will go all day without eating. She is big and sloppy and, of course, with a strong accent, coming from New Orleans. Unfortunately for her, her hair is very curly. When I went to bed last night, she had been in bed a long time, and she said she had heard people talking about her outside the window. She didn't say what they said but seemed very upset. I'll bet they said she had colored blood. Sometimes I think she has; she is so anxious to impress me that she is all white. She brags a good deal about her father's position and the fine clothes she has—but they are all in her trunk, which she hasn't opened. She's harmless, though, and I feel sorry for her.

I'm going to walk now and settle my breakfast. More later.

I have just learned something from the chief engineer. There is usually a smooth voyage like this only once a year. We are going very rapidly. At the present rate, we should be at Plymouth by Thursday noon or at least during daylight, thank heaven. I hate to reach a new place in the night.

The family whose seats are near mine and who have six small children have a governess with them who smokes and is very English looking. They are also traveling with a nurse as well as the woman's mother and father, he being a brother of Pierpont Morgan.

Apparently he likes this boat and always crosses on it. Guess you won't look down on my boat now!

The ship is certainly a steady one. I don't quite understand about this Gulf Stream. It seems to hang onto us after we think we are going to be out of it. It is cooler, however, as the water is only 70 degrees this morning.

People have just been telling me that the only vegetable I will get in England is cabbage. Cheerful prospect, isn't it?

Tuesday morning

A grand night's rest. We're out of the Gulf Stream at last. I've had my breakfast. Felt pretty bum part of the day yesterday, but I was all right when I kept still. I didn't know whether I dared venture dinner last night but went down, ate olives, bread and butter, and good baked ham. Nothing ever tasted as good as those olives! Went to bed at nine o'clock, and all is well. The English girl says it isn't true about the cabbage—that the British have several vegetables.

Wednesday

We still have good weather and are making good time. We should be in Plymouth by one o'clock tomorrow.

Thursday morning

I got up early and just had breakfast. Land is in sight, and gulls are following the boat. There are all kinds of boats in view. I'll be glad to land. Haven't decided what to do first, but will know when I get to Plymouth. They claim this is a record voyage for the *Zeeland*. We are a whole day ahead of schedule!

All of you write all about the family. Copy my address and inquire how long it takes mail to get there. Until the last of August write to me c/o American Express, 6 Haymarket in London.

As we are nearing the end of our voyage, I'll close this letter. I have finally decided after talking with the Episcopal priest that I will go to Exeter, Salisbury, and Winchester on the way to London.

Goodbye, my dear ones all.

Lots and lots of love,

Nora

Royal Clarence Hotel
Exeter

Thursday, July 26, 1923

Dear family,

I'll write a little of my letter which will go to you later. I jour-
neyed on a slow train from Plymouth today and came up here to
Exeter, the capital of Devonshire, an old cathedral town. The oldest
part of the cathedral was built in the early part of the twelfth century.

A girl on the train told me about this hotel which is really very
elegant and is right in the center of the cathedral district.

I got a good glimpse of rural England coming up on the train. It
was really very lovely. The most striking thing about it is the fact
that the fields are all divided by hedges which are like rows of trees.
I don't see why they separate little patches of ground in that way,
but they do. Where the ground is bare it is as red as brick. I saw
quantities of white daisies, the biggest I have ever seen, and the
trees are beautiful.

I am tired and ready for bed. I can't write anything of any account now, but I wish you were all here. It's so quaint and interesting.

Good night.

Regent Palace Hotel
Piccadilly Circus
London

Wednesday, August 1

I am writing to you at least part of a letter this morning. I found
this scrawl which I wrote at Exeter, a very beautiful place.

Now I can say that I spent the night right in the cathedral district with the cathedral just across the street and the bishop's palace
and all that goes with it nearby. It was very beautiful, and I'm glad I
saw it—but I can't say that I slept in a cathedral town, for their very
elegant dinner made me so sick that I scarcely closed my eyes. I'll
have more to say on English food when I reach home. Am having too
good a time to talk about it now.

In Exeter the hotel people had to put up a cot in a drawing room for me. It was a most elegant room full of old stuff, but every direction I turned I looked in a mirror and saw that bilious-looking face of mine.

I had intended to go to Salisbury and Winchester but I felt so sick, and the hotels all seemed to be full, that I went straight to London instead. This is a family hotel near the British museum.

As soon as I could I went to the American Express office where I found letters from Jessie, Clara, and Maude Evans. Then last night when I came back from a trip around the city there was another letter from Clara written July 20, and this morning one from Elva. Seems just like being at home.

Last night I read Clara's letter four times without stopping. Then I read it again before I went to sleep. Clara, you put Elva on the list for my letters after they go to Sadie, will you, please? Be sure to put in the list of names and let each one scratch off her name.

In Jessie's letter, which she had written after coming back here from Scotland, she advised me to come to this hotel, the Regent Palace, and she also had the foresight to engage a room for me. Couldn't get one for July 27 but got one for the following day.

This is an immense place right down in Piccadilly Circus near Haymarket and the American Express office. I have a room and breakfast for nine shillings six pence, and the management absolutely forbids tipping. The rooms haven't baths, but there is running water, hot as can be, and there are plenty of bathrooms. Guests are entitled to one bath a day, and I ring for it to be prepared just like any lady. I also put my boots out to be cleaned. (Clara and Sadie, you never did that for me!)

When I paid my bill at the Abbotsford it amounted to more than this hotel with the tips, even though it was a shabby old place badly run down but highly respectable with old ladies sitting about drinking tea. Felt better as soon as I moved here.

My indigestion continued, and I kept pretty quiet over Sunday— just rested and let it wear off. I feel fine now, but I try not to overdo.

Jessie advised me what trips to take first, so Monday morning I went on an American Express auto trip around the city and central London. It lasted three hours. A guide explained things to us so it would be easy to go back later to whatever we wanted to see. He took us to the Strand, past St. Paul's Cathedral and a lot of other places, but the most fascinating was the Tower of London. Although we spent a long time there on the tour, it was so interesting that I went back all by myself yesterday morning and looked it over again.

I went down to the Tower by bus. (There are great numbers of those high buses, similar to those in New York, but no elevated trains and no streetcars except in the poorer section.) By asking a good many questions I managed to get there, but it took some time as the streets were so packed and so narrow that the traffic was held up often.

I walked about the wonderful old Tower of London and looked at the very elegant guards drilling in what must have been the old moat. Some of those elegant "Redcoats" have black fur headdresses which would almost make a coat. Then I went again up and down the narrow, winding stone stairs to places where so many prisoners met their doom. I really got many thrills out of it.

In the armory I saw the gun carriage which bore the body of Victoria, the uniform worn by the Duke of Wellington, the cloak worn by General Wolfe in which he died on the Heights of Abraham. I stood in the dungeon where Bloody Mary in her religious zeal imprisoned so many. In the inner court, surrounded by tower buildings, there is an inscription marking the site of the scaffold on which were executed Anne Boleyn, Lady Jane Grey, and others. There is a brass plate with this inscription: "On this spot Queen Anne Boleyn was beheaded on the 19 of March, 1536."

As we had passed the place with our guide on Monday, he pointed out one portly, red-faced guard and said, "That is the handsomest guard in the Service." Whereupon the old fellow, who seemed to be more Irish than English, answered, "You will report at ten o'clock tomorrow for execution."

Yesterday, Tuesday, when I came out after doing all this again by myself, I ran into the American Express party with the same guide, who very kindly brought me back to the hotel so I didn't have that long bus ride.

Then yesterday afternoon I went on another American Express city trip through the west end of London. We saw many elegant residences with large yards, but many people live in houses like rows of apartments all hitched together. I suppose they have lawns in back, but they certainly have no front yards.

We went past Hyde Park, which had many sheep grazing in it but otherwise seemed to be just a great common with grass and trees. We saw Buckingham Palace and ended our tour with Westminster Abbey. Well, at last I've seen it. My head still swims from looking at the tombs of so many notables. It's a great place. I must go back to it several times.

Thursday

Last evening an English girl took me to see many interesting, out-of-the-way things which I would not otherwise have seen. It ended with a bus ride to Richmond and a long tramp by the Thames. Thought I might be dead this morning, but I'm as good as new.

I have also met some Americans at the hotel, so I'm not all alone. Am going on an all-day trip to Windsor and Hampton Court today with a girl from St. Louis. We met at American Express and decided on this trip together. She's a nice girl, but I have forgotten her name.

Clara wrote that "Nora still keeps us in touch with each other, although the ocean is between us." I am well and happy. Love to all—and I want letters.

Nora

London
Friday, August 3, 1923

My dear family,

I arose late this morning, ate my breakfast, and hurried down to American Express to be greeted with the news that the President is dead. It seems so strange to read in a foreign paper an account of the death of our chief executive. How many changes it will make in so many different circles!

Well, poor Harding; I think he didn't have a bed of roses. My respect for him increased greatly when I found that he did not consider his administration a great success, or at least he did not feel that it had been popular.

This news is too staggering. I must go out into the sunshine and think it over. I wish you would write. I miss letters from home.

Love for the present.

Later in the day, August 3

I am waiting for a California woman who is going to Westminster Abbey with me. I went through with the American Express tour the other day, and now I want to return and see it again in a more lei-surely fashion. We are going about noon in hopes of avoiding a crowd.

Later

Mrs. Warren, the California woman, and I had a good time at Westminster Abbey. Most of the statues are perfectly hideous, but if one looks up it is all right, for the architecture is surely wonderful.

After having some miserable tea near the Abbey, we took a bus to Kensington Gardens, a huge park with lovely trees and flowers. It's a great place for children, and it was there, upon seeing them playing, that Barrie got his inspiration for *Peter Pan*. We saw a little pond just surrounded by children watching the small sailboats they had sent out and the swans swimming around. What a cheerful sight it was!

The weather is beautiful, cool and bright. I wear my suit always and sometimes need more.

We are all stunned by Harding's death. It seems strange to see the Stars and Stripes at half mast here.

Later

I'll go back to Wednesday when the English girl took me for a ramble. She surely made me do some walking, and strange to say, it didn't hurt me at all.

We went to the London Museum, which is housed in an old mansion and is full of interesting things. I do wonder how they kept the ceilings clean and how they ever heated the great arks, but that was their problem, not mine. I was much interested in the court gowns of earlier times and even of the present, coming down to those worn at the last coronation. This is probably as near as I shall ever get to royalty. There were quaint clothes worn by royal children, and we saw a cradle which was used by all of Victoria's infants. Dreadful to think that they rocked their babies, and I'm quite sure they didn't feed them vegetables according to our modern, improved method. If they did get vegetables, they fared better than people do in England now. (Clara, please don't mention your garden again. I'm having such a good time that I don't want to leave, but I might have to sail for home at once if you keep enumerating those good vegetables!)

Late in the afternoon we took a bus to Richmond, miles out in another direction, but still in London. It's awfully interesting to ride up high on a bus reading the strange signs and looking at quaint buildings.

The English girl wanted me to see Kew Gardens, so we walked along the Thames from Richmond to Kew. I think it isn't much more than a hundred miles. It's been many years since I've walked so far, but I'm proud to say I am none the worse for wear. There are wide stretches of open green and mighty trees. I believe there are hundreds of deer in the park.

Kew Gardens, which we reached at last, are among the most well-known botanical gardens in the world. All sorts of tropical plants are brought in and nursed along in glass houses, then placed in the gardens when they will stand the air. I was surprised to find a mass of Oregon grapes which were labeled with some odd name and marked as coming from Turkey, I think. The trees were the most beautiful I have seen here—many firs and others of that sort. The gardens used to be a farm belonging to George III, and there was a modest palace to which he withdrew from worries. Several queens also had cottages there.

We took the underground railway, known as "The Tube," back to town and returned quickly.

The next day, Thursday, I had signed up for an American Express trip to Windsor. I awoke feeling fine but decided to wear my old ground-gripper shoes, as my feet felt a trifle stiff. We started in a motorbus with the top down so we could see everything. It was a long ride. On the way we went through Stoke Poges and stopped at the little churchyard where Gray wrote his "Elegy." It's a lovely, quiet place. We paused under the yew tree where he is said to have written his poem. That yew is supposed to be one-thousand years old.

Next we took a boat ride on the Thames. The bus left us, and the driver went on to Windsor where he met us later, while we boarded a little steamboat for an hour's ride past many beautiful country places. We had lunch at Windsor in a hotel right on the beach before touring the castle. At the castle we were taken through room after room by a guide who explained things, but we did not see any of the rooms where royalty live now. Such elegance, such magnificence! It fairly makes my head swim to think of it.

On the way back we stopped at Huntington Court. When we asked who occupied the old castle now, the guide said that most of the residents are pensioned widows. Well, the widows certainly have some very lovely grounds to wander about in. I saw the most beautiful flowers there that I have seen anywhere, as well as a perfectly marvelous grapevine with huge masses of grapes. The vine had been growing there since 1782.

Sunday night, August 5

Saturday morning I went to American Express as usual, hoping for letters but received none. Then I went up to St. James Palace to witness the changing of the Royal Guard. Those gentlemen surely are most elegant with their red coats and tall black fur hats. I didn't understand it all, but it took a long time and lots of maneuvers for one group to relieve another as the band played stirring music.

We had not been able to get into the Houses of Parliament, but someone told me that, as it was Saturday and Parliament was in session, they would be open to the public until 3:30 p.m., so I went up to Mrs. Murray's room to tell her. She got up, and we went together. I am so glad I didn't miss it.

First we entered the King's robing room where he gets dressed to open Parliament. I suppose if he throws his things around the way I do, it's all right, for he has someone to pick up after him.

The room for the House of Lords is very small, and so is the one for House of Commons. Considering the size of that tremendous building, I really don't see why they couldn't loosen up and give them more space.

After seeing the Houses of Parliament we dropped into Westminster Abbey for a few minutes. A service was going on, and the music was very fine. This morning, Sunday, I went to St. Paul's for service. I think I shall go back again later and really see all they have to exhibit.

This afternoon Mrs. Warren and I went to the National Gallery, which is only a few minutes' walk from here. It's the second time I've been there, and I enjoy it so much. I just love to sit down and study the paintings I like best.

We came back to the hotel at 4:30 p.m., and I decided to go to bed until dinner; but I wasn't sleepy, so I got out the letters I've received since I arrived and reread them all. There aren't many. Then I read all the family letters I received on the steamer and got a touch of home in that way. I wondered what you all were doing and hoped that I would hear from you soon.

And you are wondering what I think of the English. Of course, they say there are no Londoners here at this season. It's all country people and foreigners. And when I go to New York, they always say there are no New Yorkers there.

The food is strange. Mrs. Warren and I ate in the restaurant in our hotel tonight and had the regular dinner, which cost 3 shillings 9 pence, about $.90 in United States currency. We had grapefruit a little larger than a lemon, thin soup, then fish with a small potato, lamb chops with two or three green peas. (Personally, I think the peas aren't green at all, but dried.) We finished the meal with chicken and a salad of very tough lettuce which I ate because I am pining for vegetables. Dessert was ice cream. Water is not served unless asked for. The English all drink wine or other alcoholic beverages. I don't blame them. The water is warm and chalky. I myself would drink if I knew what to order, but I don't.

The people are helpful, but I find police and bus drivers a trifle vague in their directions, and I never know where a bus is going to stop.

Well, I must go to bed. I'm still crazy about London even if I do write stupid letters.

I am so anxious to hear from you all.

Good night, and love to all.

Monday, August 6

I got up and went down to American Express before breakfast as I was anxious for mail, but it's a bank holiday, and even American Express was closed. Well, perhaps there wouldn't have been any mail anyway, and now I at least have it to look forward to.

Clara, you tell Mrs. Emerson that I made lunch out of her cake yesterday, and it was very good. I surely thought of you all as I sat there in my room eating that delicious cake, but I didn't dare picture you too closely or I should have been homesick. You'll see me for a good long visit, Clara, before I go back to Spokane, if you'll keep me. This is all mighty interesting and enjoyable, but I shall want to see you all before I go back to work. Mrs. Warren and I seem to be hitting it off very well, so I'm not really alone.

Later in the day, Monday, August 6

This morning I found I was so tired that I went to bed at noon and rested and slept all afternoon. It is now five o'clock, and I'm just up, feel better, and think that a late dinner with two meat courses isn't a very good idea, so I will dine earlier and more simply tonight.

I miss all of you. Sadie, I'm anxious to hear all about your trip, and I also want to hear about Sarah Louise's trip. And those blessed kids. Tell me what they are doing. Bernice, I want to hear all about that husky son of yours. Dorothy, let me know about college life at Carleton. Lizzie, I wanted to see you again before I left but called Phyllis' place and could get no answer. Hope Phyllis is feeling better now. Charles, be a good boy and keep up your fine record in school. I shall want to know what your grades are just as I used to back home.

I'll number this letter three. The first was written on the boat, the second mailed last Wednesday. If I number them, you will know if you get all of them.

And now, my best love to you all—and remember me to inquiring friends.

Love,

Nora

York
Friday, August 10, 1923

My dear family,

My feet are tired and I must go to bed, but I can't go without telling you what a good time I've had today.

It grew very hot in London and I was glad to get away, but I wanted to hear from Jessie. Then too, I had to figure out my own plans before leaving London so I would know just what to write to her so that we can meet in Venice.

I lay awake the better part of two nights deciding what to do, then came north as far as Cambridge yesterday, Thursday. It was so hot I went right to bed and stayed there till 4:30 p.m., then wandered out; and as my hotel was near the colleges, I walked down to them. An old man wanted to act as my guide, but I didn't like his looks. Later another one whom I liked attached himself to me, and I kept him until nearly eight o'clock.

I never had much notion of what the colleges were like, but now I shall always have a picture of them. We went into two beautiful chapels, and in one place we got into the dining hall. It was a dingy-looking place with paintings on the walls and Chippendale chairs at the "quality" table. The plain fellows had benches.

I hired a boat, and my guide took me for a row down the little stream which flows right along the "backs" of the colleges. It is weedy but very beautiful with old weeping willows drooping over the banks and lovely grounds on either side. We pushed on to a turn where there were two very old mills no longer in use. There were some beautiful residences terraced right down to the stream. I can't describe it well, for it isn't like anything I have ever seen anywhere else.

Cambridge is small enough to be decidedly a college town. I stayed at the University Arms Hotel, a place full of elegant old English stuff, but I had to walk to the fourth floor and sleep in a hot room. It was so hot and they seemed so respectable that I left my door open and got a good breeze.

This morning I got up very late, went to the ticket office nearby, and found that I could make the best train connections by going to York at 11:45 this morning, staying tonight, and taking a fast train to Edinburgh tomorrow. I have a hotel room booked in Edinburgh already which I thought was a good idea, as I imagine Scotland is full of tourists just now.

From the ticket office I sprinted back to the hotel, threw my things together, and rushed for the station. I am so glad I decided to stay at York tonight. I reached here at 4:30 and went to the Station Hotel which is very good.

The town looked so interesting that I hurried up to the cathedral which is one of the most beautiful in England. The verger who took us around showed us one window that is said to have 45,000 pounds of old glass in it. The windows are beautiful. The whole thing is too majestic and wonderful to attempt to describe. I climbed to the top of the cathedral on some miserable spiral stone steps, and what a splendid view! It was clear, and we were able to see the surrounding country for a distance of fifteen or twenty miles.

York has around it a wall which is built upon the remains of an old Roman wall. My hotel is outside the wall, so if the city is attacked tonight, I suppose I am lost. A little river runs through the town, and I watched a beautiful sunset on it tonight.

Coming up today, I saw fields of grain just red with poppies—those pretty little scarlet single ones that I have always liked so much. It was a beautiful sight.

In two weeks I expect to go back to London. Then if I don't get cold feet, I shall cross the channel from Dover to Ostend and spend two days in Belgium before going to Paris. If I get leery about traveling alone, I shall fly to Paris, but I should rather like to see Brussels.

I am looking forward to spending a day with my friend, Alice Borresen, in Paris before going on to Venice where I will meet Jessie. It will surely be good to be with someone I know well. After we do Italy, we may come back and spend some time in Paris before leaving for home. Then you will have to board me till the end of January.

I have so far heard from none of the family but Clara and Charles, I mean of the letters sent to me in London. After September 1 my mail should go to Paris c/o American Express, 11 rue Scribe. Now write that down, all of you, and let me hear from you. I'll add to this after I reach Edinburgh. Good night.

Edinburgh, Wednesday, August 15

Well, here I am leaving tomorrow and I haven't written a line to you yet.

I didn't tell you much about that lovely old York cathedral, but I haven't the language to do it. It is great just to walk through and look up at a splendid thing like that and feel the awe and wonder of it. I was sorry I didn't reach there early enough for the memorial service for Harding. The Archbishop spoke. I did get a newspaper which had both his speech and the one delivered at Westminster Abbey. Both express the greatest friendliness to the United States.

I wonder what will be the upshot of this dispute between France and England. I was talking with a Princeton professor the other day who said that it wouldn't come in our time, but that he looked for a break eventually between the two countries.

I arrived safely in Edinburgh, a wonderfully attractive city with an old castle, now a garrison, which looms so high that it is an imposing sight. Princes Street just below it is very beautiful. Of course, I had to visit the castle and see the room of the ill-fated Mary, a tiny, gloomy room in which James VI was born and from which he is said to have been lowered in a basket when he was two days old and taken to Sterling to be baptized in the Catholic faith.

Then I visited Holyrood Palace, full of associations with Mary and Darnley. Saw the beds on which they slept, but like my own mattress better.

There is always a bus to jump into and take a ride somewhere, so I took a drive up around the hill back of the Palace. They call it Arthur's Seat. King Arthur is supposed to have watched a battle from there. On the way down we went through High Street, which leads to Holyrood Palace. It used to be the home of nobility and now is the very poorest slum section of the city. When the Royal family come here now, they stay at Holyrood.

When I returned from this drive, there was another longer one just starting, and I decided to take it twenty-eight miles out into the country. I love these country rides through the little villages. On the way we visited the ruins of Craigmillar Castle, much frequented by Mary.

I won't weary you with all I have done, but just want to say that today I went to Abbotsford, Scott's lovely old home, to Dryburgh Abbey, the old ruined abbey where he is buried, and to Melrose Abbey, which he loved and put into his *Lay of the Last Minstrel*. Tomorrow I will go to Glasgow by a slow route through the Trossachs.

I think I'll go to Paris to rest for several days before joining Jessie in Venice. I get pretty tired, and after leaving the cool country, I'll have to get used to the heat again. Our friend, Alice Borresen, who is living in Paris is away on her vacation but has left word at her hotel that if they have no room for me, I am to have her room— so I'll be all right. Living is cheap there, and it isn't here, so when I'm through with trotting around here, I've a notion to go to London and just fly over to Paris. It would save a lot of fuss, and the airline takes you from the field right to your hotel.

Oh, my dear people, keep well, and don't let anything happen to you. Sometimes it frightens me when I think of all these weeks cut off from all communication with you.

Sadie, if you see Margaret Fehr before I do, tell her that the money bag of which I made so much fun is the joy of my life. If I ever go abroad again, I'm going to have another one hitched to me that carries all of my baggage as well.

Do write.

Love to all,

Nora

Glasgow
August 16, 1923

My dear people,

I sent a letter this morning, but I've had such a good time today that I must tell you about it. I left Edinburgh at 9:30 this morning for the trip to Glasgow by way of the Trossachs, made famous by Scott in his *Lady of the Lake*. (Don't I sound like a schoolteacher?)

It was a very roundabout way, and I was told in Edinburgh that I had better check my grip and not try to bother with it myself. Having no faith in their baggage system, I gave it up reluctantly but put a nightgown and toothbrush in my coat pocket. However, my suitcase was here when I reached the hotel.

First we went on the train, then took a motorbus to the Trossachs Hotel where we had luncheon. Later we took a bus to Loch Katrine and a steamer the length of the lake. There we were met by a stage, a high-seated affair drawn by four horses and driven by a red-coated gentleman. I loved it all.

The purple heather is just coming out, and the hills are covered with it. I was so afraid that I wasn't going to have a chance to pick some heather, and the driver kept saying that there would be plenty near the pier at Loch Katrine. When we reached there it was raining, but a Scottish gentleman, admiring my zeal as we drove through the land I know so well from reading Scott, walked with me up the hill and cut me a whole armful of it.

Later he and his quiet little wife took me under their wing, and she gave me sandwiches, real homemade ones that tasted like something. It was a wonderful day, and I loved every minute of it, but it rained quite a bit toward evening and now has become very cold.

I am staying tonight at the hotel right at the station, a fine one too. When I registered I met two nice girls from Arkansas, and we ate dinner together. It seemed so good not to eat alone.

Well, two weeks from tonight I shall probably be on my way to meet Jessie. If it weren't so cold and rainy I would stay and take a trip on the Clyde, but I think I shall go on to Keswick in the Lake Country instead.

Good night. I just wanted to let you know what a wonderful day I had.

Lots of love.

Keswick

Sunday night, August 19

It is 9 o'clock and I've just finished supper, so I'll write a few lines before going to bed.

Since Friday I have been in the lake region of England made famous by the Lake School of Poets. The mountains here are covered in places with purple heather, and the foxgloves are glorious. In an area of about thirty miles England has gathered all of her lakes, and it is really very beautiful. Keswick, pronounced "Kesick," is situated on Derwentwater, the most beautiful of the lakes.

I came here without a booking and took my chances on a hotel. At this season of the year everything is usually full, but I was able to get in. I have a tiny attic room with only a skylight for a window, but it's comfortable, and I much prefer it to a cot in the drawing room. Then too, it was cheaper, and I was glad of that, so I just settled down here and will stay until tomorrow morning when I plan to go on to Chester.

I have had a wonderful rest here, and the people are homelike and kindly. It's very quiet, in an old-fashioned stone house with a big garden full of climbing roses, rhododendrons, and other lovely flowers.

The food is good, and I've eaten more here than anywhere else in England. Since today is Sunday, we had breakfast at 9:00, dinner at 1:00, tea at 4:30, and supper at 8:00. For tea they served bread and butter, jam, cake, and something that I would call pie, but I suppose they call it a tart. For supper we had cold meats, salad, tea, and dessert.

It has been very cold and rainy here, but people just put on raincoats and go. I have worn my suit with my heavy coat over it most of the time.

Yesterday I went by bus to several places of interest past some of the lakes, through lovely woods, and finally to Windermere and Bowness, which is just beyond, but also on Lake Windermere. I took a boat ride on the lake, which is larger than Derwentwater, but not so beautiful.

We also stopped in Grasmere to see Wordsworth's grave and the little vine-covered cottage where he used to live. On the way back we visited Wythburn Church, one of the smallest churches in England. It was heated by two tiny stoves and was as quaint as could be.

Coleridge has a poem about it in which he says that only God himself knows whether he is not more pleased with it than the impressive temples built in his honor.

What a wonderful rest it has been to come to this quiet, peaceful bit of country with its real scenery. Everything has been interesting, but I'm a bit tired of dead kings.

I hate to leave this nice, homelike hotel, which doesn't seem like a hotel at all. There is even a kitten here. We sit four at a table, and last night I happened to be seated with three such nice people—an Englishman, his wife, and a young Swiss friend of theirs. They are traveling through the country on motorcycles and stopped here for the weekend.

This noon they were out on a hike, and some people who were here just for dinner sat at my table. They were talkative and very interesting. They speak hopefully of settling the affairs with France peaceably and say that the English people object very much to a break with France. They are concerned for the tremendous army of the unemployed here, and they speak kindly and sadly of the awful amount they owe us.

My dear family, I pray every night that you may all keep safe— and it will be a relief to get to London, where I hope I shall hear from you. You will know it if anything happens to me, but I'm afraid I shouldn't know if anything happened to you.

I think I shall write to Ruth West and the faculty at Lewis and Clark, so you needn't send Ruth this letter or any after this.

Queen Hotel, Chester
Monday evening, August 20

Well, here I am in probably the oldest town in England. Whatever I should say about it would sound like a guide book, so I had better not say anything except that I've had a little walk around, and the buildings are surely the quaintest I have seen. This was one of the principal military stations of the Romans. I walked for a distance upon the city wall tonight and came to the tower which bore the inscription, "Here Charles I stood during the Battle of Rowton Moor and gazed on the defeat of his army, September 24, 1645." From that point I could see such picturesque signs as "Ye Olde Nag's Head Hotel" and "Ye Olde Coach and Horses Hotel."

This morning proved that I'm not fit to travel alone. I marched down to the station to take the train to Chester, when upon examining my ticket just in time, I discovered that it called for a bus ride from Keswick to Windermere—so I had another nice ride through the Lake Country, got to Windermere at 1:00, had lunch, and took the train at 2:15 for Chester.

It was cold and rainy when I arrived. In the coach this morning an Englishman next to me said to his wife, "Isn't it strange that Americans think this is cold. They surely have it colder than this in New York." I suppose they think we have just one season.

Tomorrow I shall get up early and explore the town and then go on at noon to Stratford.

Stratford-on-Avon,

Wednesday, August 22

Here I am in Shakespeare's old haunt, and I'm happily disappointed in it. I am not the only one who feels this way. Other people I've met haven't seemed to care for it so very much either.

Tuesday morning I spent walking around Chester. The wall makes a complete circle, so if you ascend the stairs to the top and continue walking, you come back eventually to the place where you started. If you ask about distance here, they always say it's five minutes' or ten minutes' walk, so when a woman told me it was an hour's walk around the wall, I was a little leery about it, but I pinned down a practical looking man, and he said it was a mile and a quarter. Anyway, it was an easy walk for me. (Clara, you tell Mr. Evans that from one point I looked over to the mountains of North Wales, but I didn't see any of his people, although I thought of him and looked hard.)

The country in Stratford is as green as it is at home in the spring. This month there will be plays in the Shakespeare Memorial Theater done by the excellent Shakespeare Players, so I knew beforehand that the hotels would be booked.

When I got off the train, a taxi driver came up to me and asked what he could do for me. I said, "Tell me if there is any place in this town where an American woman can lay her head." Whereupon he said, "I'll take you to a nice temperance hotel, Lady. You leave it to me." He took me to a pleasant looking place, but they were full and suggested another private hotel. A very attractive young woman runs it. I liked her at once. She said she could take me for a night and then she had promised the room to some ladies who were coming the next day. It's such a relief not to be managed by a lordly hotel porter who always seems to think he is ever so much more important than the Prince of Wales!

Best of all, there is an American girl here, a teacher from Cornell College in Iowa. She came over with some friends, had the mumps, and is having to rest while they go on. They put us at the same table, and we've been together all day. We have all of our meals in the house, and it's much cheaper than a real hotel. Sometimes I think I never want to see a big hotel again. Miss Mills, for that is her name (and she looks like Beulah), was going to the theater last night, so I went too and saw *Much Ado about Nothing*. The actors are so remarkable that I went again this afternoon to see *Macbeth*. We will most likely go again tomorrow night.

After the theater we walked down to the church where Shakespeare is buried, and I really did get a thrill as I stood over the place where he lies. I'm glad his bones are here and not in Westminster Abbey.

This morning we walked over the fields to Ann Hathaway's cottage. I hope Shakespeare went the same path we took, but I'm not certain of that. It was a bright morning, and the thatch-roofed cottage is most attractive. It has been kept more like a dwelling house than a museum, which is a relief after seeing so many relics piled together in places of that sort.

Tonight the ladies who were to have my room came, so I have moved into the home of some dear old ladies, but I go back to the other place for meals. I have a nice big room that looks out on the garden and is as quiet as can be. Have decided to stay here till Saturday, for I love it. I'll stay over Sunday in Oxford, go to London Monday, and to Paris Tuesday.

Lots of love,

Nora

Cosmo Hotel
London
Friday night, August 24, 1923

My dear people,

Yesterday I had a sudden urge to get my mail, so I left Stratford in the afternoon and came on to Oxford and to London this afternoon. Tomorrow I'm going to "fly" to Paris. I won't mail this till I get there. Then you'll know I'm alive.

Emma Clarke from Spokane had studied at Oxford and lived with a woman whom she wanted me to look up, so when I arrived in Oxford yesterday and it was raining hard, I just took a taxi to the address she had given me. Here came this sweet-faced woman to the door, and she took me in. I had such a nice time with her. I really enjoyed it more than Oxford itself. She said she hadn't much in the house, but if I would be content with a simple supper of bacon with bread and tea, she could look after me.

As you can probably tell from my letters, I'm dead sick of lordly hotels and porters, so I try to look for less pretentious places managed by real people.

In spite of the rain, I went out to see one of the colleges and walked down to the river. It was pouring when I got back, and Mrs. Money put my coat and shoes in the kitchen to dry by the stove. Then she served me supper in the little sitting room which belongs to the "lodger" who is there when classes are in session at the university.

It was cold, and English houses are beastly cold—no heat but tiny fireplaces that wouldn't keep a chicken warm. I took a hot water bottle to bed with me and had a fine night's rest.

This morning it was bright, then rained a little, and then cleared up. I spent the forenoon visiting the colleges, then came on to London where I found a nice bunch of letters waiting for me. You see, I've been away two weeks, and I was beginning to get anxious to hear from you all and from Jessie, too, to know just what we are going to do in Italy. I opened Jessie's three letters first so I would know what I should do next to get things arranged with American Express. I am to find out just when I'll be in Venice and then wire Jessie, and she'll make her plans accordingly.

I'm sure my hotel is all right, or they wouldn't have sent me, but I'm not awfully keen about it. Made up my mind I might as well go on to Paris the quickest and easiest way, so I'm flying. Had thought of going through Belgium, but this dashing through places is hard work. However, I am going through Switzerland, and I'm going to Paris and just rest, absolutely, for a few days. It sounds strange to go to Paris to rest, but Alice Borresen told me to go to her hotel, and if they hadn't a room, they were to give me hers. She is on vacation and will be back Tuesday, so I'll just lie around until she comes, wash my hair, get my clothes cleaned, etc. It will be a rest just to know I don't have to take a train the next day, and I'll get along somehow.

How I did enjoy reading your letters! I heard from Clara (two letters), Sarah Louise, Blanche, Deb, Dorothy, and Margaret Fehr, who was keeping house for the Ginders while Sadie was away. It was wonderful to hear from all of you, and I'll enjoy reading your letters a dozen times more. Bless you all! Write again soon.

Paris
Sunday night, August 26
I'm sure you'll think me crazy, for I've about decided that I like Paris better than London, though I haven't been anywhere yet and have had an awful time communicating with people. I've had the grandest rest today that I've had in a month.

But let me go back to yesterday when I "flew." I was mighty glad to leave that hotel. The taxi called for me at 11:30 a.m., picked up some other people, and took us all out to the "air station." It was a comfort to take a good long ride in a taxi and know that I wouldn't have to pay for it.

One man who was with us in the taxi bought a bunch of white heather, and I thought then that he was buying it for luck. He later admitted that was true. There was another woman, an American, and she and I were together until Paris. She says she has a daughter who went crazy in war work and is at a private sanitarium just outside of Paris. The woman is rich and has everything done for her. She goes to see her daughter often and says that her case is absolutely hopeless. I couldn't help thinking how much easier death would have been.

Well, at the air station they examined our passports, weighed our baggage, and stowed us away in the plane. The front was partly partitioned off from the rest and held four people, a man named Jack and a woman, the lady on her way to visit her sick daughter, and I. All the other passengers were men, with the exception of a young mother, her little girl, and tiny baby.

We started at last, and after we had gone a little distance I noticed that one of the engines had stopped. I thought maybe that was the regular thing, but our pilot turned the plane around and took us right back to the field from which we had started. We had lunch there and fooled around, and finally at 4:30 p.m. they called us. It was the same machine; they had just doctored up the engine. I think none of us felt overly confident in it, but I wasn't afraid.

I'm glad I made the trip. I timed it, and we were twenty-two minutes crossing the channel. It is a sensation to go flying over towns and fields. There seemed to be no farmhouses, but all of the farmers live in villages nearby.

Just after we crossed the channel, we noticed that we were going down again, and we had visions of spending the night out there in a field, but they were only stopping to let a few people off. When we got to the Paris air station, they examined our passports but didn't even look at our baggage.

We were taken to our hotels, and I wished then that we had arrived by daylight, for I knew that Alice Borresen would be gone until Tuesday. The taxi driver seemed to have some difficulty finding the hotel, which is in the Latin Quarter—but at last, there was the sign, and I trudged up some dingy stairs to find a man at the desk who couldn't speak a word of English. I told him I was a friend of Miss Borresen, but he didn't understand my pronunciation and protested he knew her not. Finally I persuaded him that he did know her, and he gave me a room.

I came to Paris to rest for the Italian trip, so today I stayed in bed till 2:30 p.m., and I surely did rest. Then I went to the Luxemburg Gardens which were nearby. It was such a lovely park, and I enjoyed watching the people. Most of the men were reading, and the women were sewing or crocheting. I moved around and sat near different groups just for the sake of studying them.

I think tomorrow I shall go to American Express to fix up my trip through Switzerland, but I shall do no sightseeing. I still need to rest, and we shall have time for that later.

I've just read all your letters again and enjoyed them so much. I was glad to get your picture, Clara, and I think it is fine. Of course, I don't think mine flatters me. Blanche, I was so delighted with the picture of little George. Sarah Louise, that was a fine letter, and I thank you for the pictures of Blanche and the girls. Deborah, I enjoyed your letter, but am sorry you haven't been feeling well. Was so glad to have that visit with you and shall certainly see you on the way back. Dorothy, when do you go to college? I have forgotten, and you didn't say. Lizzie, Mabel, and Jennie, I haven't heard from you, but I love you just the same. Jennie, dry a little extra corn for me. If you knew how I have starved for fruits and vegetables!

Isn't it strange that I don't feel a bit lonely here where no one understands a word I say? It must be because of your wonderful letters.

Paris
Wednesday, August 29

Well, I certainly have done my share of resting. Am so lazy that I must have needed the rest.

Alice Borresen came home late last evening and came to my door before I was up this morning. It was so good to see her. She is busy working on her doctorate at the Sorbonne and had to study this morning. We went to lunch and then to American Express where I found letters forwarded to me from London. Sadie, did I tell you I did receive Mrs. Evans' letter and am sorry that I didn't get around to seeing her mother, but distances are great and I'm rather stupid about finding my way.

I will go to Switzerland Friday morning and meet Jessie in Venice on Wednesday, September 5.

I have post cards of England to send but have been too lazy to write them. Maybe I'll do some tomorrow. Write to me at 11 rue Scribe, Paris, c/o American Express.

Love to all,

Nora

Montreux, Switzerland
Friday evening, August 31, 1923

My dear family,

This morning I left Paris at 8:20 and was on the train until after 8:00 tonight, arriving in Montreux where I will stay until tomorrow morning before going on to Interlaken and then to Lucerne. This town is on Lake Geneva.

I let American Express fix up the trip for me. I have a book of railway tickets and another book which covers my lunch today on the train, my taxi to the hotel, and takes care of the hotel bills and everything else along the way. Of course, all of this costs more than it would to arrange it myself, but it's a relief not to have to take care of any of the business part in a foreign country whose language I do not speak.

I was dreading the long day on the train, but it turned out all right. The trains are like those in England. You are shut off into little compartments. There is room for eight, but there were only three of us all day. I was with two sisters from Philadelphia, awfully nice women and great travelers. What a good time we had together!

We saw a lot of quaint little French villages and farms along the way. Then as we neared Switzerland the scenery became rugged and very interesting. We were detained for some time when we crossed the border, but they didn't make us open our luggage. I have just one piece with me, my suitcase. The other ladies had trunks and had to declare that they had no tobacco, but they didn't even bother to ask me about that.

I am feeling good after my long rest in Paris and am mighty glad I took the time to do it. I'm sure I will enjoy the rest of the journey more because of it. It does seem funny to have been in Paris for five whole days and not have had curiosity enough to see anything. There will be time for Paris later, though.

It evidently rained very hard here today. I do hope it will be nice tomorrow, but I will have to make the best of it if it isn't.

We had a delicious luncheon on the train today. Maybe you would like to know what it was. When I sat down at the table there were dishes of salad and plates of thin slices of chopped meat loaf. The salad was some kind of fish with heaps of fine mayonnaise, and it surely was good. Then the waiter took our plates away and served a ham omelette and later, a course of veal, fried potatoes, and cauli-flower. Next came a delicious, soft creamy cheese, then grapes and green almonds. I looked at the menu to see how much the lunch cost; and it was 10 francs, about 60 cents.

It's 10 o'clock, and I think I had better go to bed. I've really had a very pleasant day. Won't get any mail now for a long time, but I'm going to give you Alice Borresen's address in Paris, and in case any-thing happens, you can notify her.

Good night.

Interlaken

Saturday night, September 1

Guess I am getting lazy, for I seem to prefer looking out the win-dow at beautiful scenery to bestirring myself in any way. I should have stayed in Montreux long enough to go to the castle, the Prison of Chillon, but I didn't. Anyway, I'm tired of being thrilled by look-ing at places where people suffered. I want to see beautiful things that are right and happy, so I took a long, lovely ride on an electric train through the Swiss mountains—not so grand as some of our own scenery, but there is that wonderful green which we don't have. The mountainsides are one rich, green carpet, and there are many flowers—little things sticking up through the grass just like lavender crocuses in our own lawns.

The houses and barns seem to be built right together with win-dows few and small, usually with wooden shutters. I'll venture the natives breathe very little of this good air at night.

I have met a nice couple from California. Mrs. Lutz is about my age and her husband considerably older and retired. His hobby is his auto. He has driven several times across the States from coast to coast. His wife says she has gone along to please him, and now he is taking this trip to please her. She has a tremendous amount of en-ergy and is very good company, so I was glad when I found we were going to the same hotel in Interlaken. We arrived in the middle of the afternoon and took a short tour together in one of those little rigs driven by a horse. We have decided to go to Lucerne together tomorrow afternoon, and then we may do something else here in the evening, although there isn't a great deal to do unless one makes quite a long trip. I had intended to leave Lucerne Tuesday, but I guess I'll stay till Wednesday and let Jessie get to Venice two hours ahead of me on Thursday.

I have been out for a walk along the shore of Lake Geneva. My hotel, which is very grand indeed, is right on the shore of this lovely lake. I have a few minutes before going to my train and wanted to get a little exercise. The town lies just at the foot of a mountain. It is wonderfully lovely, and the lake is a very clear blue.

Later

I'm on the train now, but it will be some time before it leaves. I'm glad to be here early and get a good seat, for I want to see all there is to be seen.

The Swiss are regular robbers on their prices. I wondered how they managed to hold me up for more than American Express had paid, but I fully expected them to do it. Always in Switzerland baths are 65 cents, that is, baths with a towel. I really don't know how one would manage a bath without a towel. Well, for some reason they put me into a room with a private bath, and I tell you I took a good long soak. I supposed, of course, they would charge me for it, but they didn't, until I was leaving that is, and then they added two dollars to the bill!

Lucerne, Tuesday morning

If the sun hadn't come out bright and strong Sunday morning, I should never have believed that the Swiss mountains were as grand as the Canadian Rockies, but luckily for Switzerland the sun did shine, and there was the Jungfrau in all its glory, a magnificent sight. We went up the mountainside about three-thousand feet and it was some view!

Mr. and Mrs. Lutz and I traveled on to Lucerne Sunday afternoon, and the ride there was even more beautiful than that to Interlaken. We were booked for different hotels, but they promised to look me up so we could go somewhere together. As luck was with us, their hotel almost joins mine, and our rooms look out on balconies just a few feet apart, so all we have to do is call to one another from our balconies.

Our hotels hang right out over the Meuse River just at the entrance to the lake. The meals are excellent. This is the loveliest place. I wish I had words to describe it, but I will try to tell you about it when I see you.

Yesterday we went for a long boat trip, practically the length of the lake. Mr. and Mrs. Lutz are going to cut their stay here one day so they can go to Milan with me tomorrow. I'm so glad, for we can look around together there Wednesday night and Thursday morning.

This morning was a sight indeed—market day. It was worth more than a dozen art galleries. Throngs of people, and I saw what I wanted to see—people who weren't dressed up and on parade but just out doing the family marketing or selling their wares. We saw masses of fruit and many kinds of cheeses and vegetables. It surely is a happy change from England. After remembering the market, I now find myself hungry and anxious for a meal.

Later

I've had my lunch, and we are soon going out again on a long train ride. The mountains are wonderful here—the highest in Switzerland, I suppose, and they say that Lucerne is the most beautiful lake. I'm so glad to have someone to travel with. I tell you, I will appreciate Jessie when I meet her.

Wednesday morning, September 5

Here goes for the last lap on this letter, as I am going to take the train soon. I feel like a new woman, for this wonderful Swiss country has made me over. I think traveling with friends has probably had something to do with it too.

Yesterday Mrs. Lutz and I went for two train rides. At the end of each was a cable line we took up to a high point which afforded views so beautiful that we almost wanted to stop the clock and look at them forever.

You know, I flew on Saturday on the French line. The following Monday there was an accident on that same line. One man was killed and all of the others on the plane injured. Glad I didn't go that day.

Last night we went to an orchestra concert. It cost 10 cents in American money, and the music was fine. Of course, people here are brought up with music from an early age. We came home late and explored some of the narrow streets. I'm so glad Mr. and Mrs. Lutz are with me in Milan, for we can go out in the evening, and if I were alone I couldn't.

Just think—my school is opening this week, and I won't be there. Well, I'll have a good long visit in Minnesota before I begin work. Put up lots of fruit, all of you, and don't forget me.

You see, I number my letters so you will know whether or not you get them all. Clara, when you write, I wish you would say what date you received the last letter and its number. I always write in my diary the date I send the letter.

I think about you all so much, and when I return to Paris, I shall hope for lots of letters. Write to me at American Express, 11 rue Scribe, Paris.

Love,

Nora

P.S. Well, here goes for sunny Italy. I'm scared stiff of the fleas and mosquitoes, but one can always leave.

Bertolini's Hotel Europe
Milan
Wednesday night, September 5, 1923

Dear family,

Well, here I am in Italy. We left Lucerne this morning in bright sunshine and rode through the most beautiful countryside. The Swiss mountains and lakes are surely winners. When we weren't going through tunnels we looked out the windows every minute of the time.

There was quite a delay in crossing the border when they made us all get out of the train. We hadn't had to do that when we entered Switzerland from France. However, when I started to open my suitcase for the customs official, he motioned to me to not to open it and just put the stamp on it without looking inside.

I mailed letter number seven this morning, and if you don't get it, it will probably be because I didn't tip the postmaster!

Mr. and Mrs. Lutz have gone to a different hotel but are coming after me this evening, and we are going to see the town. After getting in about 5:30 this afternoon, I cleaned up and had a good dinner, and now I'm waiting for them to stop by for me. As long as I'll be here only until 2 o'clock tomorrow I can afford to overdo a little.

The cathedral is just a few steps from our hotel. We passed the famous Italian Lake Como on our way here, but thought it not so beautiful as the Swiss lakes. The Italian countryside through which we passed didn't look so very different from the countryside at home. The people seem terribly polite here, but I have heard they will steal you blind.

Tuesday night, September 11

I really didn't think it would be so long before I would write again, and now here I am in Florence. I shall have to go back to the point where I stopped which was last Wednesday night in Milan.

My hotel was very fine, but my room was right on the street downtown. In fact, I could open my windows, walk out on the balcony, and take in all of the life of the street.

We went out after dinner and strolled around for awhile. Just across from the cathedral there is a huge arcade said to have cost one and one-half million dollars and considered to be the finest in the world. It is under a dome and is surrounded by shops and cafes. Brilliantly lighted, it is a favorite promenade in the evening.

In the morning we took an interesting sightseeing tour. After tramping around the day before, we were relieved to get into a car and be taken places.

I left Milan at 2 o'clock and at 7:30 arrived in Venice. The journey was good, and I had Italians in my compartment. They were very nice to me, and one who could speak English interpreted for me when the others spoke.

Jessie's sister, Marian, is with us here, and the two of them were all settled at the hotel when I arrived. Venice is surely like nothing else under the sun. It was dark when I arrived, and I had to get into a gondola all by myself to get to my hotel. I had supposed the hotel would not be far from the train station, but it seemed to be an awful distance, and all the narrow, dark canals looked so forbidding. I finally decided my gondolier was taking me far out of the way and began yelling "Grand Hotel" at him. He would try to reassure me that I was going there, but I began to fear that I was going to be robbed and murdered. Whereupon, I wept silently and began to wish that I were comfortably back in America. Then I got a little mad and I yelled, "You are not taking me to the Grand Hotel!" But at last I arrived, and there were the girls sitting on the porch waiting for me. Heavens, what a relief it was to see them!

I didn't care for Venice that night, but the next morning I loved it. We poked around and saw things for ourselves and then took a gondola ride in the afternoon. Saturday we took a sightseeing trip

Nora Frye in St. Mark's Square, Venice, Italy, 1923.

and did things a little more thoroughly. There are some magnificent churches in Venice which we enjoyed, but best of all we liked the picture made by sky and water and the colorful buildings. It is something to remember all one's life. I didn't sleep much there, but that was partly because the gondoliers were singing all night just outside my window. There is netting over the beds in Venice, but the windows are without screens. I found two or three mosquitoes, but I have seen no fleas. It was cool enough to sleep under a blanket at night.

We had to smile about the way they try to hold Americans up and think they are surely going to make us pay for the War. We lunched at a sidewalk cafe in Venice, and you would have laughed to see our bill. They charge, of course, for service. Then there is a tax and a charge for the tablecloth and for bread, although we hadn't asked for bread. We had to pay for it just the same.

The weather has been hot here in the middle of the day, and I usually wear a dress and no wrap instead of my suit.

Sunday morning we had to get up at 4:30 to catch our train for Florence. It was pitch dark at first, but by the time we were in our gondola there were streaks of dawn and it all formed a beautiful picture.

We reached here about 1:00 p.m. Sunday and after a little haggling with the baggage men, took a taxi to our "pension." Personally I like it much better than a hotel. There is no lordly head porter to treat you like the dirt under his feet. An English woman runs the place and I like her. There are also some very nice people staying here. I like the Italian people too. The servants stand whenever we pass them and are usually smiling as they work.

Our building is right downtown, just across the street from American Express and is an old palace fortress, whatever that means. There are great, high, gloomy rooms and walls probably two feet thick, but it is very clean and the meals are pretty good.

I'm all over the indigestion that the English food gave me and must say I like French and Italian cooking much better. We get fresh fruit for dessert, and I'm surely enjoying the ripe figs. It's a joke about the water. People tell us we must not drink water in Italy, and every place we have been so far they swear that the water is fine, so I drink it. I've tried to drink their wine but find it poor stuff.

They say that summer this year in Florence was hot, and it is very dry and dusty. There are no blankets on our beds—only sheets and spreads, and before morning I sometimes have to put my coat over me. We have not seen mosquitoes here so far.

Of course, Florence is rich in art galleries and old churches. We toured one great gallery yesterday afternoon and another this morning. We really should go back again, but we aren't staying long enough for that.

We are close to the great cathedral here, and just across from it is what they call the Baptistry, a very old building. While we were there yesterday, a very elaborately dressed infant was baptized. The way the priest poured the water on the poor little head was frightful. Jessie said, "Just think! That cold water!" But I assured her that there was little danger of its being cold. At least we have yet to find any cold water in Italy.

This afternoon we took a streetcar and went out three miles to the old town of Fiesole, which is on a high point and commands a fine view of Florence and the surrounding country. It was good to get up high, as the air seemed better than in Florence, which is much lower. On the way we passed many vineyards with grapevines twining around the branches of trees and great clusters of grapes hanging down in a most inviting way. In Fiesole we went to a museum and saw relics dating back to 800 B.C. But best of all, we enjoyed looking over the great expanse of country with monasteries dotting the landscape, each on its solitary hill.

I surely love the South, and if the fleas and mosquitoes will behave as well as they have so far, I shall be perfectly happy.

We leave for Rome on Friday, so I'll send this letter off to you before we go.

Good night.

Nora

Rome, Italy
September 15, 1923

My dear people,

We had a pleasant trip from Florence to Rome since it was cool and there were no others in our compartment. We passed through miles and miles of vineyards where the grapevines were tangled and twined around the trees. The stone farmhouses here look so plain and cheerless, unlike our farmhouses.

We arrived in Rome about 3:30 in a pouring rain. As Florence was very dusty, we were all glad to see the rain but were afraid now that it had started it might keep up indefinitely. Our pension was near the train station, but we decided to take a taxi because of the rain. Then there was the usual row with the driver. You read his meter, but that doesn't seem to have anything to do with what he demands. It was quite a circus to see him rave and throw his arms around. Marian is for being firm and standing for her rights, while Jessie is for avoiding a scene. Finally after Jessie gave him about twice as much as we thought we ought to pay, he threw the bill tragically on the ground and drove off.

Always when we go out to buy fruit here it seems just as high as it is at home. People say they put the price up for Americans, and I think they do. As we aren't very successful in beating them down, I have bought very little. I wanted to buy you all some nice presents, but if I do I won't have money to go home on, and you will have to bail me out to get me back—so I will probably buy you pocket handkerchiefs in New York. I'm such a poor shopper anyway, and I have to spend so much energy to do it well. I just can't bear to tear myself away from all that there is to see in order to go shopping. (This is just to warn you that I'm buying nothing, although I should dearly love to bring you all kinds of nice gifts.)

We are at another pension here in Rome, the Girardet, where the food is better but we aren't given so much. At other places we have had so many courses that when we first came here we didn't know enough to load up. I have a fierce appetite after sightseeing all day, so last night I took great big helpings and got filled up. I thought in England I would never be hungry again, but French, Swiss, and Italian food is a different proposition. In fact, I am rapidly regaining the pounds I lost in England in spite of our strenuous pace of activities.

Our pension here is attractive and as clean as can be. The people working here are mostly Italians, but the signorina who runs it speaks English fairly well. I have a hard time trying to communicate with the maids, but as I don't want much, I get along. I'm glad I washed all my clothes in Florence, for there I found the hot water tap and got all I wanted. Here we are each allowed one pitcher a day of hot water. By the way, when we arrived the signorina asked, "Is it all the same name—a mother and her daughters?" So you see, I don't always look like an old maid schoolteacher. I surely don't feel like one with September here and my not being in school.

We have breakfast whenever we please, and it's always a continental breakfast with rolls and coffee. I have hot chocolate. I got to drinking it in France and Switzerland where it is whipped and served with an extra pot of hot milk for mixing it as one likes. Here it isn't so good, but it is more nourishing than water. Lunch is served at 1:00, and dinner at 8:00. It seems that dinner gets later and later as we go further south.

Yesterday we went downtown in the rain to American Express where Jessie got some mail that had been forwarded, but I was so afraid that they would ball things up that I'm not having mine sent on from Paris but will look for letters from all of you when I reach there the last of the month.

From American Express we took a streetcar to the Vatican Gallery on the other side of the Tiber next to St. Peter's. What a strenuous morning! Our time is so short that we were sure we could go only once, but there is such a mass of wonderful things to see. One could spend many days studying the Sistine Chapel with all of the great paintings on the ceiling. Finally we were able to get mirrors and found that we could walk along and see the paintings without straining and twisting our necks. It was thrilling to find the originals of the great pieces of statuary that we have seen only in casts. There are long, long colonnades filled with beautiful works of art which were totally unfamiliar to me. One area displayed all along the walls tapestries designed by Raphael, and the richness of their beauty was a feast to mind and eye.

In the afternoon we were so tired that we just wanted to ride and be taken somewhere, so we took a tour out on the Appian Way. It was a rest and a relief, but we have decided we can find things for ourselves in the city, have the fun of studying them from our Baedeker's, and save money. On the Appian Way tour the visit to the Catacombs of St. Calixtus was the most interesting. We were given candles and escorted through by a monk, a dear old fellow who spoke English well. We went down only two levels, but I believe there are four or five, and he explained inscriptions and decorations along the way.

On Sunday we picked up a Miss Christy at our pension, and she spent the day with us. She is a New York girl, alone and awfully homesick. We liked her very much. We all went to Sunday services at

St. Peter's, and Miss Christy and I stayed until nearly 1:00, as we kept finding more and more things of interest. It always surprises me that in the cathedrals guides and tourists pay no attention to services that are going on but walk right into the most sacred places and examine things at their leisure.

Mr. and Mrs. Lutz, the people who were with me in Switzerland, were also at our pension; so Sunday afternoon we all got a guide and visited the Forum, the Palatine Hill, and then the Colosseum by moonlight. Our guide was a young Italian woman whom we enjoyed very much. Interesting as ruins and tourist attractions are, the people always interest me more, and when at the Colosseum our guide made a statement which a bystander disputed, I enjoyed hearing them argue it out. They didn't rave and tear their hair like ignorant cab drivers, but they were just as excited, and the way they quoted different archaeologists to each other was very entertaining. I will have to read more about the Colosseum to find out which was right. There was almost too much to see for one day, but Marian needed to get over the border into France at a certain time to send the passport on to her husband in Vienna.

Part of our day on Monday was spent in seeing the lovely Pantheon. You know, it is circular and is lighted only by an opening in the center of the roof thirty feet in diameter. The effect of that soft light was very pleasing.

Toward night we took a carriage and drove to one of the hills surrounding the city for a beautiful view of the sunset. Then the driver took us all the way back to our pension. It was interesting to drive along the narrow streets and see the people in the doorways of their poor little houses. One wonders how the children ever live to grow up.

Tuesday was our last day here, and Marian was possessed to see the Pope. Miss Christy also wanted to go. Jessie and I were willing to see him but not so enthusiastic. At the American Express office they said it was impossible to get in without a permit, so after finding that the man who gave the permits was gone, we gave it up—all but Miss Christy. She took a chance, fell in with some other people who were told that it wasn't possible, but they persisted and all got in. When Miss Christy joined us later she was certainly jubilant, and Marian was just sick to think she hadn't gone.

We reached Naples at 9:30 at night after a trip through beautiful vineyards and towns built upon high points. The trees in northern

Italy weren't so very different from those in our own western states, but here it is quite different with palms and lemons, figs, and other fruit trees. I love it all, and I hope you won't get sick of my raving about it.

Naples was a real hubbub when we got there after dark. We had two hotels in mind but found that both were full. Then followed a mix-up among the boys representing different hotels and the fellow carrying our baggage. I was wondering what they were going to do with us, but Jessie found that the Vesuvius Hotel could take us, and there we went. When we got into their bus after all that jabbering, a nice-looking man said, "Well, this looks like a party of Americans." He proved to be from St. Paul, Minnesota, and was lots of fun. His wife said she has spoken broken German, French, and Italian until she is sick of it and that when she sees the lady holding the torch in New York harbor she is going to kiss her.

Well, the old volcano itself couldn't have beaten the racket we heard all night long outside our windows at the Vesuvius, but it's all in the day's work when you are traveling in Italy.

We went by streetcar the next day and visited the ruins of Pompeii, which we enjoyed very much. Then we decided to go to Sorrento, so we had to take a carriage to a place called Castellamare and a streetcar from there. We met all kinds of fellows who wanted to escort us, and we had a most amusing time which ended by our being taken in a cart pulled by a horse for less than half the price most of them demanded. It was a very entertaining drive, for going with a horse and cart we had time to see so much more than in a motor vehicle.

The tram ride to Sorrento was also lovely, up the hills and along the bay. We stayed at a beautiful hotel, and if we had had sense enough to spend the next day there, all would have been well, but we took a boat to the island of Capri. I want to save that adventure to tell you about in person, but it was one great day! Don't forget to ask me about the trip to Capri and the Blue Grotto.

We came back to Naples that night and on to Rome yesterday where we had two hours before taking the train to Pisa. We arrived at midnight and are leaving very soon. We'll stay in Genoa tonight and then go on to Nice tomorrow.

I was awakened early this morning by a terrible hubbub under my window and got up to find that there was a market right below my room, so I put on my coat and hung out the window to watch the people, for they were much better than a movie. Later I went out to the market to buy some fruit, but the whole place looked so dirty I changed my mind. The hotels are very clean though, but if I don't have a real drink of water pretty soon I will die.

Goodbye for now.

Love,

Nora

Nice, France

September 25, 1923

Dear family,

It is six o'clock at the end of a beautiful day, and I'm sitting on the rocks right close to the sea listening to the waves roll in to shore.

For fear that some of you may have as vague an idea of the Riviera as I have always had, I'll explain that it is the Mediterranean coast along this part of southern France and northern Italy and is very beautiful.

I think I sent my last letter from Pisa. We went from there to Genoa where we merely spent the night but had a very good hotel. Going from Genoa to Nice we had to cross the border, and there was all that fuss. My suitcase was jammed full, but the beast made me open it and he pawed around quite a bit. I was afraid I might never get it shut again if I once opened it, but I did, with the help of a porter who was seeing us through.

Today I acquired a suit box and shall use it for the overflow. I had some difficulty getting it. It seemed to me that every place I went into, they either didn't have boxes or didn't speak English, but finally I found just what I needed.

Our trip Sunday along the Italian coast was very lovely, but we went through so many tunnels that we didn't see as much as we wanted to. After we crossed the border, there were fewer tunnels and we were glad to be able to enjoy more of the countryside. The mountains run right down to the sea, so there was a succession of beautiful scenes. We passed many palms, olive groves, and handsome villas. Happily our hotel in Nice is right on the sea so we can just throw open our shutters and take it all in.

Yesterday we went for an all day sightseeing tour, but we stopped for two hours for lunch at a border town and an hour at Monte Carlo. We had to show our passports there, as Monaco is an independent principality. Someone told us that we would not be allowed into the casino if our passports showed that we were teachers, but we got in all right and watched the people play. I didn't envy any of them, for they were so intent on winning that they didn't look very happy.

We have done nothing strenuous today, and I have sat by the sea most of the time. It is so lovely that I hate to leave, but we must go tomorrow; so I won't write any more at present.

Goodbye.

Later, September 25

Well, the joke is on us. We wanted to break the journey to Paris and couldn't quite decide what to do, so we finally agreed to come to this little place, stop off tonight, and if it looked at all promising, to stay another night and take a trip tomorrow. When we got nearly to Marseilles, we almost decided to get off and spend the night there but didn't. We continued on, thinking that we would surely land in the wilderness, but we would try it anyway. It was dark, nearing eight o'clock when we arrived, and when we reached our hotel bus we found it full of people. We were driven up to the swellest-looking hotel we have seen for some time, with an orchestra playing and a good restaurant. We have now finished a delicious dinner and are going to arrange for a trip tomorrow.

We have just heard of the big fire in Berkeley, and I'm so anxious to know if Blanche was burned out. I hope some of you will think to write me about what is happening. Otherwise, I will worry until I hear.

I am getting anxious to get to Paris and get my mail. Won't I be disappointed if there isn't any!

Paris, Saturday, September 29

I awoke in Paris this morning very tired and very cross. In fact, I thought I would take the next train home and just cut out Paris, but now I'm feeling better. I've had a shampoo and have been to American Express and picked up my mail, so I think I'll stay a little while.

Several of your letters had been sent to England but were forwarded. I got more than a dozen, mostly from family. While the other girls shopped, I tagged along and read my letters. Oh, but it was good to hear from all of you! I just devoured them—and wasn't it good that they came when I most needed something! There were also three fat letters from Ruth West at school.

There is no question that we have been going too hard, but we'll take it easier now. I expect I will never have as good a time as I had in Italy, but maybe Paris will be just as interesting. Whatever happens nothing can take Italy from me.

Love to all.

Tuesday, October 1

Well, here I am at American Express waiting for a girl who sent me a note that she was in town. I found it with the rest of my mail when I arrived, but as she didn't date her letter, I have no idea whether she is even in the city. She probably left two weeks ago, but I'll wait a little to see if she comes.

The last letter I had from any of you was Clara's, written September 8. It seems as though there ought to be more mail by now, but there isn't.

Yesterday we all moved, and I feel a little more settled now. You remember, our friend Alice Borresen is studying here and has been in Paris for two years. She has naturally had to live economically and is at a hotel in the Latin Quarter—cheap, humble, reasonably clean and respectable. When we arrived at the hotel, there was only one available room and that a double one, but she got me a room in a hotel nearby, and the other two girls took the one at the St. Louis.

My room was terribly cheerless and I felt awfully alone. The room the girls had was right on a front street and so noisy they couldn't stand it. They managed yesterday to get a room in a better hotel nearby, but there was none for me. However, a room was suddenly vacated right next to Alice's, on a quiet side of the house, so I took it. Last night I got unpacked and put away the clothes I had rescued from my trunk which is still at American Express. When I went to bed I really felt quite at home.

Marian's husband comes day after tomorrow, and they are to sail for home on the fourteenth. She is scouring the town for clothes, and as I don't love shopping I have just gone sightseeing on my own.

Yesterday I walked a long distance slowly around and through the Place de la Concorde which is one of the largest and most beautiful squares in the world. This was the location of the guillotine during the French Revolution where Louis XVI, Marie Antoninette, and some 2000 others lost their heads. Taking in the beauty and the history of the place I wandered down great avenues of horse chestnut trees which have turned reddish brown.

I am beginning to get a thrill out of Paris. We were so tired when we got here and it was so noisy that I think we all felt a bit homesick. I was surprised when I looked at my watch yesterday to find it was nearly six o'clock. I was dead tired after all of my wandering around but really had a most satisfactory day.

The Association of College Women has a clubhouse here not far from where we are rooming. After Marian leaves, Jessie and I are going there to live, as it is a much better place. We went up there to dinner last night and liked it very much.

This morning I took the guide book and poked around by myself, finding all kinds of interesting landmarks. Met the girls downtown for lunch, and now as soon as I finish this, I'm going to find an American library and get something to read.

This is a pretty poor letter, and I'm so sorry for Clara that she has to copy it, but I can't do any better now.

And now goodbye and lots of love to all.

Write.

Nora

On the train between Paris and Cherbourg
October 31, 1923

Dear folks,

I've been lazy about writing to you lately because I knew I would be going home soon, but I'll write one last "round robin letter" from France on the train. Anyway I have postage for a letter and I can't afford to lose it, so I want to write to you before I'm out of France in the morning. This will probably go on a fast boat and reach the States before I do.

When you see that the *President Adams* of the U.S. Line has landed at Hoboken you'll know that I am safe. It will probably be Saturday night, November 10, but may not be until the eleventh.

If you haven't forgotten me, I would love to hear from you all. I will probably be away from New York before this reaches most of you, but you might write to me at Mapleton, and Clara could forward your letters if I'm not there. I had letters from Clara, Sadie, and Elva recently but haven't heard much from the rest of you.

Paris is so lovely I hate to leave it. When we first came up from Italy, it seemed so cold, rainy and cheerless, while Italy had been sunny and warm. But we got some nice weather after all, unusually nice, they say, for this season of the year. I do like Paris very much, and I would rather leave when I want to stay than be glad to get away from it. Anyhow, I'm coming back to Europe sometime before so very long. Maybe some of the rest of you will be ready to come with me then. It would be much easier a second time, for I would understand so many things that I have had to learn by experience. But it has all been great and very much worthwhile.

Life at the American University Club was so pleasant that I would hate to go to a hotel from there, and that is what we would have had to do now that the college girls are coming back. We certainly had splendid accommodations for what we paid, owing to the endowment made by Mrs. Whitelaw Reid. It's so much more restful to be in a place that you know is clean. It's strange how dirty many places are over here and how one gets used to it after awhile.

Today was a drizzly day, but yesterday was the most perfect autumn day. A girl at the hotel and I went to Sainte Chappelle, a lovely little chapel in the Palais de Justice, an old royal palace with this gem of a chapel still as it was hundreds of years ago.

Then we went into the law courts which we found very interesting. There was a big hall where people were either sitting or walking about, the black-gowned lawyers talking with their clients. There were several women lawyers in the crowd. We got into one room where a case was being tried. I can't understand French, but the girl with me explained it. A man had been run into by a truck. It was fun just to watch them talk even if I couldn't understand what they said.

Taxis are absurdly cheap here, and I indulged in three of them today before our train left at 3:40 this afternoon. First I went to a big department store to get some things I wanted. As there were several little things, I just kept the interpreter they gave me, walked around the store, got what I wanted, and then paid for it all at once. One item was a rubber shower cap. U.S. Lines give a great deal for your money, and we will have a private shower. I wanted some safety pins, but they sell them only by the box—a big box of the poorest things you ever saw. Then I wanted some common pins, but they come only in a tin box like a pepper box. Too much baggage. I had to give it up. My next stop was at a chiropodist's office. I found one the other day who does fairly good work and is very cheap. But I didn't go there because she was cheap. It's right in the best part of town, and I had heard that she did good work. The girl trimmed me up well, but I have a feeling that her implements are never even washed. However, after all this walking it was a great relief. Next I scurried to a hairdresser and got a shampoo. Some of the hairdressers here make no pretense of being clean, but this one was fine, and I will start off with a clean head.

We are to be guests of the steamship company tonight. As we sail so early it is necessary to stay in Cherbourg all night. U.S. Lines pays the hotel bills and have also just brought us each a box lunch so that we don't have to eat on the train. Jessie was hungry and ate hers right up, but I'm going to wait, as I'm afraid the evening will seem too long if I eat early.

We have been to a good many operas and theaters, of which there seem to be plenty in Paris. Consequently, we have been up pretty late nights. One night we stopped to get something to eat before going home and found that we were too late for the subway at the station where we transferred, so we had to get a taxi, which wasn't easy to do in the part of the city where we had become stranded. Finally we flagged one down and got back to our hotel.

We had to laugh about Marian, Jessie's sister. At every place we went this fall she would see something she wanted, go away without buying it, and then have regrets because she didn't get it. Meanwhile she would miss getting things in the place where we were and regret it in the next city. When we reached Paris she was crazy over the shops and said that now she was going to have her own way and do all the shopping she pleased. She was determined to have some Paris gowns and ran around seeing dressmakers. That is how they do it here. If you want anything good, you go to a dressmaker, see a model you like, and order a dress just like it. Marian did order a dress from Alice Borresen's dressmaker. I fully intended to get one there too, but thought I would wait until Marian had her fitting. I wish you could have seen it. It looked as though I had cut it myself! Marian was so disgusted that she gave the woman the half she had deposited and left it. Then she ordered two others somewhere else with no deposit. Neither of those was done when she left, so she went home without a Paris gown. She had also ordered a fancy silk handbag made, and that didn't come either. When she reached home, she ca-bled Jessie to bring her an umbrella, two pairs of gloves, and two bottles of perfume. We had a good laugh over that cable.

Finally I got ambitious and began looking at ready-made dresses, thinking that they might have some good-looking ones, but I couldn't find any, so I guess I'll just have to get something in New York. I did get a hat. It isn't anything special except for the price, but it will save me that much agony in New York. The milliner made my hat, and I think I went at least half a dozen times for fittings. I hate shopping for hats so much that I'm just glad I have one and won't have to bother any more about it. I got a new umbrella too. I suppose I ought to have picked up many more things, but there was so much to see that I just couldn't bear to spend my time in shops.

Jessie had a lovely dress made, but she didn't know until the last minute whether she was going to get it. I think they finished it about fifteen minutes before we left Paris. We stopped on the way to the station, but it wasn't done. Then they actually brought it to the train for her.

There are six of us in this compartment on the train, all going on the same ship. I wonder what kind of a voyage we will have. I can't hope to have it as smooth as it was coming over. It isn't often like that, but I hope at least it will be fairly smooth.

Our train is moving at a very slow pace, and I think it will be midnight when we arrive. The box lunch was good—a large hunk of bread without butter, cold ham, roast pork, Swiss cheese, a banana, a bottle of water, and a bottle of wine. It was all right, but somehow I don't have that satisfied feeling that I have when I eat a picnic lunch at home. (Clara, are you and the Evans family good enough sports for a winter picnic when I get home? A big rousing fire would feel good, and stuff cooked over it would taste so good.)

We just found out that this poky train will arrive at 11:45 p.m., not a cheerful prospect when the tender will have to meet the boat at seven in the morning. There is a bright spot, however. It seems they give us dinner when we get there if we want it.

Love,

Nora

President Adams, U.S. Lines
Friday, November 2, 1923

My dear family,

Well, here I am, enjoying the sea immensely again. It's cold, but I think it is more beautiful than in summer.

Leaving Cherbourg for our ship was a dismal affair. It seemed to me that I was barely asleep when they called us. It was pouring rain and colder than Greenland. We had a hurried breakfast, then went on to customs. Happily the baggage inspector asked us only if we had any gold. Then we rushed for the tender, which took us out to the *President Adams*.

On the way to our ship a very voluble man from Pennsylvania regaled us with his ideas on Prohibition. He told us also that when Wilson came over to Europe he brought fifty walking sticks, and his wife brought one-hundred-fifty gowns. Well, anyone is welcome to travel in Europe with a lot of clothes if she wants to, but I know how I am going next time. Don't be surprised at that next time, for it is going to be. Incidentally, this trip has driven away all lurking notions that my time might come soon. My fear now is that I may outlive you all.

I did so enjoy the day on deck yesterday. There is a glassed-in deck and also an open one. I started with my chair on the enclosed one but soon had it changed to the other. It was cold, but I put on all the clothes I have and just enjoyed it.

I am glad this is an American ship. The meals aren't as elaborate as they were going over, but they suit me much better. I confess I don't like going into the dining room on a ship. Last night the sea was a little rough, and the room was pretty hot. After dinner I went right to our cabin and dropped upon my couch. Didn't dare budge for a time. When I finally did move, I just took off my clothes and got into bed. I slept like a log and got up this morning feeling wonderful. I wanted to be up early to see Queenstown, where we took on passengers. We didn't land. Rather, the passengers were brought out to the ship on a tender. I can't say that this coast is very scenic, but at least now I've seen it. Several women with lace and things to sell came on shipboard from the tender. One of them was full of Irish blarney, and the things she called out to the men were perfectly killing.

This is a very good ship—not so dressy a crowd, not nearly so smart a crowd as on the *Zeeland*, but very interesting people. So many of them have been to Japan and China and other places. Jessie and I have a roommate who is an author, a Mrs. Parker who used to live in Seattle. She wrote *An American Idyll*. She lives in Switzerland now and is on her way to New York to see publishers about a new book she is bringing out.

The gulls which have followed us from Queenstown, a great flock of them, are staying with our boat. We had nothing like that going over, but I once saw such a flock in Minnesota on Lake Superior. It's getting cloudy and rainy now, and the officers have been telling us dismally of their awful trip over. I wonder what is in store for us.

Thursday, November 8

Well, it's a strange life. Today I'm sitting on an open deck, bareheaded and enjoying a lovely day. The sea is as beautiful and charming as a sea can be, and I love it all. Yet only forty-eight hours ago I was hating it with a bitter hatred and swearing I would never make the crossing again. Yet we've had no really bad weather. One day, according to the chart, was rough, and that was all.

I began to get sick Friday, and I was good and sick. After I was all over the dreadful nausea, I was so weak and wretched that I felt almost as bad as before. I managed to stay on deck all but one day. That was the day I couldn't sit up. Enough of that!

Yesterday morning I felt almost like myself, and today quite so, but you won't catch me going into the dining room. Instead I have my meals brought up on deck. And mind you, they haven't had to put on the table rails, close portholes, or otherwise batten down the hatches. Guess I'm always bound to sail on a calm sea. Well, it can't be too calm for me. The wind was against us at first, but now we are sailing right with it, and they say we shall be in New York on Saturday. Yesterday we had fog all day, and the fog horn kept blaring from early morning till late at night. Today, though, it is warm and sunny. I don't understand where this warm weather can come from in November.

I am not sure how long I will stay in New York. I do want to see the sights, for I don't know when I will be there again. If I can find an inexpensive place to stay, I would like to spend some time there, but alas, as my funds are running low, I may be able to stay only a few days.

I am probably the most antisocial person on board this ship. I just want to lie and rest, so that's what I do, not going to the dining room, not dressing up, and going to bed very early. I just sleep and sleep. Our cabin-mate is very jolly and nice. Fortunately the three of us all agree on fresh air. There are two portholes and we have them open all the time.

Guess it's time to give my eyes a rest, so goodbye for the present.

Saturday morning

It's such a glorious day, and we are to land in New York tonight. Thursday night was the Captain's dinner. Everyone dressed up, and we were served a very elaborate meal. I half thought I would go down, but I was just too lazy, so I had my turkey served on deck. Last night, however, I did dress up and go down and stood it very well. Then I stayed down for the concert. My, but it was an unfortunate affair. The entertainer had spent $6,000 in Europe having her voice cultivated and had splendid testimonials from her teacher. Honestly, the poor thing couldn't sing much better than I can. I felt sorry for her. Perhaps she had also been a victim of seasickness.

The sea is so lovely now, I just must look at it. I'll mail this when we get in, and Clara, please send it on to the rest.

Saturday noon

We have just sighted land. I'm not sorry, and I'm not hilarious over it. To tell the truth, I've had such a good rest on this boat for the past few days that I would just as soon continue.

Saturday evening

Well, we've been "getting in" for the past three hours and are not through with the formalities yet. They have inspected our passports. The doctor has inspected us, and we were told to look him in the eye. I couldn't see that he did anything, but they said he could tell if we had trachoma or whatever that awful eye disease is. Next they are going to feed us. In fact, the first shift is eating. Then we will report to the customs officers. I have an idea they will make short work of us.

The harbor is beautiful with its many islands, and there is a new moon which I saw over my right shoulder. Guess I forgot to tell you that we don't land in New York but in Hoboken. I suppose some taxi driver will be willing to take us across for an exorbitant price. It's all in the day's work.

Guess I'll keep this letter until we get to New York and find a hotel so you won't picture me still floating about.

Sunday morning

I have just had breakfast and will write a note. We landed all right, and New York harbor was the most beautiful thing I have seen in the past four months. I had seen the Statue of Liberty at night, but it is different when you are approaching from a distance. I can't imagine a more wonderful greeting for foreigners than that brilliant figure with her flame held high. The lights in the tall buildings made New York look like a city on a hill.

We passed through customs without any difficulty. Of course, I didn't have anything to declare anyway, but that doesn't prevent their throwing everything out if they want to. I guess I looked poor, for the man apologized for making me open the trunk at all.

We left our trunks to be expressed over, got a porter to take us to the subway station, and after a short trip by subway under the river, found a hotel. The air was so oppressive in our hotel room that I slept very little.

Monday morning

Yesterday we were so tired and unsettled, but this morning I feel better. The first night our hotel was on 11 Street, but last night we stayed at the Allerton up on 57 Street. This is a very nice place and has one floor given over to the Vassar Club. As Jessie is a graduate of Vassar, we managed to get in here, and we can stay if we want to. Jessie had her trunk brought up, but I thought I'd look around for a day. It's a very nice place, but I can see $3.40 a day for a room soon eating up what I have left.

Sadie Oppenheimer called up and asked us to tea at the Civic Club, then suggested we go out to dinner together. She lives down in Greenwich Village, which is that old part of the city near Washington Square that is a favorite haunt of struggling artists and all sorts of strange people. Rents are high there, but there are lots of good places to eat and it's an interesting part of the city. She and another girl from Spokane have an apartment there.

Last summer when I was going through New York I met a girl named Miriam Bailey whom I liked so much. She wrote me a very nice letter which I got on board ship. She lives on 11 Street, and on the way to dinner I ran over to see if I could find her. It was a lucky move for me. She has a four-room apartment and is going to rent me a room. It's small, but it's quiet and opens onto a garden. (These city street noises are awfully hard on us country people!) She says I can get my breakfast in her kitchen. I am just as pleased as can be and will move over to her place today.

I tell you, New York looks so good to me! My only worry is that I may roast, as the houses all seem so hot.

Write to me at 53 West 11 Street c/o Miss Miriam Bailey. Clara, you don't need to make a copy of this letter. It really isn't valuable.

Love to all,

Nora

CHAPTER 31

Vachel Lindsay Letter

Sunday, March 7, 1937

My dear Margaret,*

I was so glad to hear from you and was surprised that you are to graduate from high school this year. Time does slip by.

As to Vachel Lindsay, I'm afraid I can't help you very much with material for your essay, but I'll gladly tell you a few things which may help you to understand better what his biographers say.

I never really got very well acquainted with Vachel. Of course, I met him, but I never felt near to him. Elizabeth Conner, his wife, was a very dear pupil of mine, and later when she came back to Spokane to teach, we were good friends. I was always fond of her and anxious that she have a chance to do what she so longed to do—go to Greece to study.

But Elizabeth came from a poor minister's family. Although her mother was a hard-working woman, there were other children in the family who needed help, including twins who must have a college education. So all in all, I was glad when Elizabeth "flew the coop" and married Vachel. I knew that life would be hard for her, but at least it would be different.

Elizabeth had one grand trip east in which she was entertained by literary people who were able to recognize her great ability and honor her accordingly. With a certain set of people here, a group which had made much of Vachel before his marriage, Elizabeth would always be just an obscure minister's daughter to be patronized and advised. I was glad that she had the trip and that Sara Teasdale sent her a lovely shawl as a wedding present. By the way, it is said that Vachel once wanted to marry Sara Teasdale. She doubtless understood his impractical ways because she left money in her will for the education of Vachel's daughter. On rare occasions when Vachel had $100.00, he was just as apt to leave it in a taxi as do

*Letter to great-niece, Margaret Gray.

157

anything else with it.

Elizabeth was teaching here when she and Vachel were married. She was one of a little group of girls to whom Vachel had paid some attention. I didn't even know that he and Elizabeth were more to each other than casual acquaintances.

One evening at the novel section of AAUW, Elizabeth reviewed *The Green Hat*. As always, she did a masterful piece of work. There was no sign of hurry or confusion. She sat down for a little while after she finished at about 8:30, answered some questions in a leisurely way, and then left before the meeting was over.

I wandered around town with some friends and reached home at about 10 o'clock. A few minutes later, Ruth West called up and said, "Nora, Vachel and Elizabeth were married at 9 o'clock this evening."

I said, "Say that again." She repeated it, and I was struck so dumb that she feared I had fainted.

Well, there was great consternation over the situation. People seemed to feel that there was unseemly haste—a girl married in her everyday clothes and a man married in a black shirt. There were three or four more weeks of school, and married teachers weren't allowed in the system. Some of the parents whose children were in Elizabeth's classes objected to having a splendid teacher replaced by a substitute, but she had to go. It seems too absurd to be true. There was pressure from a woman on the school board, a worthy soul and really a valuable board member, although her face always made me think of a composite of the WCTU. Of course, people had appealed to her sense of decency. Some of them had brought their children up carefully, and how could the board consider having a married teacher on staff, even for a few weeks? I never could quite make out what the objection was, but I must tell you a little sequel to the story. Because married women may substitute, Elizabeth was succeeded by a young, inefficient looking Mrs. who finished out the school year for her!

I spoke yesterday with Elizabeth's mother, Mrs. Conner. She said Vachel's dominant traits were affection and sensitivity. She said that he was often misunderstood because when his feelings were hurt, he would do something abrupt which looked like rudeness. Mrs. Conner was very fond of him and he of her.

Vachel also had a hot temper, which perhaps was one of the contributing causes of his final breakdown. I shall never forget one exhibition of that temper. We had hired him to speak at one of the general meetings of the AAUW. But I'll go back a little.

Members of a certain club in Coeur d'Alene had once or twice consulted me about a dramatic reader for their big guest day. A woman whom I didn't know had written to ask me to suggest someone for that event. She said they would just as soon have a book review. They could pay only $20.00. As we knew the Lindsays were pretty hard up, someone suggested asking Elizabeth. We knew they would be charmed with her and that it would be good for her to get away from the children and do something of that sort. So Polly Weaver and I went to call on the Lindsays and broach the subject. That was one time when I did have a free and easy time with Vachel, for he was in an especially happy frame of mind.

At 4 o'clock they were eating a meal. They didn't know what meal it was, but it was just a meal. Polly and I sat on the davenport. Every few minutes Vachel would rise from the table and jerk our davenport this way or that so that he could see us more clearly.

Finally, I gingerly made the offer to Elizabeth. She said she was all out of touch with that sort of thing and suggested they take Vachel. Now, some people had such feelings against him that I didn't know whether they would want him—so I parried. I said they could pay only $20.00, but Elizabeth said he would go for that, and anyway it would pay the milk bill. But I said it was a women's club, and I would have to find out whether they would take a man. Then I wrote to the Coeur d'Alene woman and suggested that she come to AAUW Saturday as my guest and decide whether she wanted him. I slipped in my card, which she was to present at the door.

Well, that meeting has gone down in history. Vachel had evidently had a very unpleasant interview with the "twelve rich men" (as he called them) who ruled Spokane. So he burst into a perfect tirade against the powers of Spokane, calling them "twelve fat spiders" and I can't remember how many more names. Occasionally he got around to the subject upon which he was supposed to talk, but every once in a while he would break out again. Actually, his real subject didn't get much attention, although we were paying him fairly well for his time. As a bit of invective, though, it was a grand piece of oratory. I was broad-minded enough to feel that while it wouldn't hurt us, it would relieve his feelings.

After the meeting was over, the Coeur d'Alene woman found me and thanked me—said she wouldn't have missed it for $100.00. They took him, and I heard that he made a splendid speech.

I can't help adding a bit of comedy to this. Ruth West was so upset by Vachel's display of unbridled emotion that she got to crying after the meeting. Finally we calmed her down and started for home. She is a thrifty soul, and as it was her week to cook, she felt that she must take advantage of a sale at a cut-rate store. She asked for a pint of cooking oil and then burst into tears. We have never found out just what were the feelings of the clerk.

I told Ruth that Vachel's display of temper didn't disturb me in the least—that I was used to quick-tempered people and felt that they got it out of their systems in that way and didn't suffer as much as we slow-tempered people did. That evening I felt that I was right when Vachel came happily into the hall to attend a dramatic meeting and waved to some of his friends in the gallery, as carefree as a schoolboy. And he didn't mention the episode to Elizabeth. She heard it from someone else.

Vachel was very kind and sympathetic toward young people. Elizabeth had belonged to my little school club of writers, the Papyrus Club, and she wanted to entertain us at their home. The students read their stories and criticized one another's work. I couldn't help feeling how kindly sympathetic Vachel was in all of his comments, always finding something to commend. One story was read which seemed to me perfectly impossible. He commented on one word in the opening sentence which he thought was especially good.

Vachel loved the movies, and some good ones he would see over and over, centering his attention on a different feature each time.

In your study of Vachel you will read of his idea of the poem games. That seemed to be his hobby, and he would have friends improvise dances to express the ideas in his poems. One time he even had a little professional dancer work with him in public performances. She was a good dancer, but I never thought she had mind or soul enough to interpret the poems.

Last summer when I was up at a cabin owned by Elizabeth Fish, after the other girls had gone, some of us were there together for a few days. Miss Fish had always been curious about those poem games. One of the girls brought in a book of Vachel's poems devoted especially to that phase of his work, and nothing would do but I should chant them and the dancing teacher dance them. And that girl, who was not at all familiar with Vachel's poems, caught the spirit of them and gave wonderful interpretations with lovely dancing.

I have always been especially fond of "The Chinese Nightingale," and one night we persuaded Vachel to read it. He liked to read his poems aloud, but didn't so much like to read those which had been written in a different mood long ago. He said it was like wearing a hat you had owned and liked fifteen years ago.

Elizabeth, poor girl, was a little hampered while he lived. I really think he didn't much want her to write because she was the young wife and must be sheltered and guarded.

After his death, she went back to Mills College to get her doctorate and teach. She is now at King-Smith Studio School, a school for girls, in Washington, D. C.

It is well that Vachel went out when he did. For some reason he seemed no longer able to do creative work and was broken and unhappy.

I once heard a literary man speak of Vachel as having something of the religious strain of the "American Victorians," but his was a different religion. He was truly religious by nature, in the best sense of the word.

And now, my dear, please don't look upon this as the work of an English teacher. I have jotted things down in a jumble, as I have had to hurry.

I hope you like "The Chinese Nightingale." Read it aloud. You have to read it aloud, as you do "The Congo."

Perhaps you would like to have one of Elizabeth's Christmas greetings. Anyway, I'm sending you one.

Lots of love,

Nora

CHAPTER 32
Letters to a Niece

Polson, Montana
September 12, 1943

Dear Beulah,*

I have thought of you so much recently, and my heart has gone out to you in your sorrow. We wished that we might have been near you to at least try to help you in our poor way.

My dear, you have been wonderful, and I admire you for the bravery and sweetness you have shown, though you knew that your little son could never be well. As I near the close of a long life, I am more and more convinced that "it isn't the living that counts, but the courage one brings to it." And your little boy didn't live in vain, for I am sure you are a stronger, more sympathetic character than you perhaps otherwise might have been.

On Tuesday, September 14, I join Clara at Missoula, and we go on to Spokane. I have had a wonderful visit here with Elizabeth and the children and have enjoyed every minute of it.

I wonder if your schools have started and if Charles has already begun his "adjecation." How I should like to hear his report of it all. We did so enjoy his visits with us when we were in Berkeley. And we were so glad that you came to see us in Spokane.

I have had a good summer and soaked up much sunshine. The weather is delightful here now. I dread the winter, but my chief concern is for us to finish this awful war.

I should love to hear from you after I return to Spokane.

Lots of love to you and Art and Charles.

Sincerely,

Nora

---

*Letter to niece, Beulah Frye Leavell.

October 22, 1944

Dear Beulah,

It's a dark, gloomy Sunday after many days of bright, rather warm weather. The fall coloring has been unusually lovely. Sometimes the leaves don't seem to put on those brilliant hues. Two weeks ago we were taken for a little drive—an event in these gasless days—and going through Manito Park we saw a tree of the most unusual red. I don't know what it was and had never seen anything just like it before. Well, all the nice days shorten a long winter, and we'll just have to be thankful for what we have had.

I love to hear you tell about your baby. He must be adorable, and Charles is fast growing up. How nice that your mother could spend so much time with you. I do hope Art was more successful on his last hunting trip.

Sarah's letters have been very interesting lately. I'm glad she enjoys the beauty of that tropical region and doesn't find life too hard.

The war seems to be buzzing right along. It's terrible to think of the boys we are losing, but it would be worse to think we allowed these terrible barbarities to go on without doing something about it. I hope and pray for leaders to rise up after this war with vision and courage enough to work for international peace. If the next generation has to go through this, I shall not rest easy in my grave. There is so much talk about prosperity that I sometimes fear that politicians place it above these precious young lives. I still insist that a better world is coming out of it all; otherwise I couldn't stand it.

Your letters always give me a warm, comfortable feeling, for you never fail to ask us to visit you. You don't know how I should love to accept. When you talk about your country being dry and parched for so long, I feel that it would be a good place for me. I'm still hoping that someday you can find me a place to board in Lincoln or near there, and I'll come and try out the climate. What fun it would be to be near you and your family without being a burden to you. I've no idea if there is such a place, but it doesn't cost anything to dream!

Will you tell me what has become of your sister Elizabeth? We haven't heard from her for ages. Maybe she has forgotten us, and maybe she is just busy. Well, anyway, with all your cares, you find time to write, and I certainly appreciate it.

Love to all,
Nora

September 28, 1945

Dear Beulah,

I was so glad to get your good letter and think you were very generous to write when you had that lovely lake to gaze upon. How nice that you could be there. I have very pleasant memories of my visit with you there. How glad I am that I have visited so many lovely places and can think about them now when I can't go places.

I was just on my way to the dentist when your letter came, so I stuffed it in my bag and opened it while the girl was getting me ready. Then I asked Dr. Brown if he knew Gordon Gilbert. He said he did and he was a very fine fellow.

Sarah seems to be very happy in New Guinea. I'm so glad. It surely must be lovely, and it's nice that she and George are within hailing distance. Such weird things I've read about the cannibals on that island. I never put much stock in them until I read in a government bulletin on New Guinea that they prefer female to male meat, and the choice slices are from arms, legs, and breasts. Just think of all the "points" Sarah would bring. It's awful to have a war, but as long as there is one, I'm glad Sarah and George are seeing an entirely different part of the world.

I've been reading a book I like so much. It's a Welsh story of the time of 1880—*The Captain's Wife* by Eiluned Lewis. You won't hear it talked about, but if you should get hold of it, I hope you'll read it. It's very wholesome, not at all like so much of the modern stuff. I was asked to review a book and have chosen it.

Do write as often as you can. I get out very little and love to hear from my people.

Love to all,

Nora

December 8, 1945

Dear Beulah,

Do you mind if I answer your note with a Christmas letter? Rather early, but it will escape the rush.

I want to wish you all a very happy Christmas and a New Year that will bring you the new house. You are wise to start all over again and build just what you want. That seems to be the only way one ever gets enough room.

Nice of you to think of me when you had an enjoyable drive. I shall never forget the day we found the poppies. It is quite wintry here now, but I have resolved not to whine about spending the winter in a cold country, much as I hate it. I think no one ever liked the outdoors more than I do—but I have many things to be thankful for.

I've been doing some tutoring lately and am greatly enjoying it. Ruth West asked me to take a boy who graduated from high school two years ago and has just returned from overseas. He wants to go to college and has had so little English that he was afraid of the placement test. Ruth seemed to be the only teacher who thought he knew anything, and they certainly gave him an inferiority complex, which I am taking out of him. He knew no grammar but is working hard and learning much. He writes beautifully of experiences overseas, so I find him most satisfactory.

Now, my dear, this is rather a poor excuse for a letter, but it is full of love.

A very merry time to you and Art and the boys.

Love,

Nora

Biographical Sketch: Nora Frye, 1867-1946

Nora Frye was born April 3, 1867, the fifth of eight children of Daniel Lee Frye and Sarah Graffam Frye who were married in Corinna, Maine May 17, 1855. Her parents were pioneers and farmers who settled on land along the banks of the Mississippi River in 1855 near what is now the community of Elk River in Sherburne County, Minnesota. Nora's parents first lived in a sod house and later in a large two-story frame house on their farm.

The eight children of Daniel and Sarah Frye were Franklin Lee Frye, born in 1856, George, in 1859, Harry, in 1861, Ida, in 1865, Nora, in 1867, Willis, in 1870, Clara, in 1873, and Sadie, in 1878. All lived into adulthood, with the exception of Harry, who died before age two while his father was away from home serving with the Union troops during the Civil War.

Nora's father was a charter member of Union Church in Elk River, which was founded in 1871 by the Reverend Jotham S. Staples, a Baptist minister whose daughter, Elizabeth, later married Nora's older brother, Franklin Frye. Eventually Nora and several members of her immediate family joined the Episcopal Church, and she remained an Episcopalian until her death.

Clara Frye, 1895.

Franklin Frye, 1890.

Nora Frye, about 1885.

Sadie Frye, 1903.

Willis Frye, 1932.

George Frye with daughter
Elizabeth, 1901.

Nora received her education through eighth grade in the Elk River Public Schools. It seems likely that her father's love of the classics in literature stimulated her interest in learning and her desire to continue in school. Later when she decided she wanted to pursue a teaching career, there was still no high school in Elk River, so Nora studied on her own, passing an entrance examination at the University of Minnesota which allowed her to complete the sub-freshman year program. She then entered the four-year university program and in 1891, at the age of twenty-four, Nora was one of two women in her class of about fifty to graduate with a B.A. degree, having earned high grades in Greek, Latin, English, history, political science, and interpretive reading. Her major was Latin. Nora had received financial help toward her education from her brother, George Frye, and later she was to help a number of her younger relatives finance their university educations. In later years she also lent money to a nephew to finance a business venture.

Following graduation from the University of Minnesota, Nora taught in small towns in Minnesota from 1891 through June of 1908, beginning her career in Rushford in a school with about fifty students. There she taught eight classes a day including Latin I, II, III, and IV as well as algebra, physiology, and astronomy.

After one year at Rushford, Nora accepted a position in Chatfield, a small town near Rochester where the people were largely conservative and relatively wealthy. She remained in Chatfield through June of 1897 when she moved on to Litchfield where she taught during the Spanish-American War.

Gleanings from the newspapers of that time suggest that Miss Frye was a well-liked teacher. The *Litchfield Independent* reported on October 25, 1898 that Miss Frye's Latin students had stayed after school until dark the previous Friday reciting Cicero. On November 1, 1898, the *Litchfield Independent* reported that the girls in the high school were very pleased that Miss Frye had volunteered to teach them Delsarte during their physical education classes as a substitute for soccer, which they hated. Delsarte was a system of calisthenics designed to teach poise to young ladies. It was developed by a French teacher of music and dramatics by that name and combined singing, declamation, and dancing.

After leaving Litchfield, Nora taught in Stillwater until 1908 when she moved west to Spokane, Washington. There were no openings in Latin when she went to Spokane, so Nora began teaching English at Lewis and Clark High School and continued in English for twenty-nine years until she retired in 1937 following forty-six years of teaching. While at Lewis and Clark High School, Nora served for many years as adviser of the Papyrus Club, an association for aspiring young writers. One of her students and club members was Elizabeth Conner, who later became the wife of the well-known American poet, Vachel Lindsay.

Disappointed in love as a young woman in her late twenties when she was teaching in Chatfield, Nora remained single all of her life, devoting her energies to her career and often spending her vacations taking courses or demonstration-teaching in summer training programs as well as visiting with friends and family members in California, Idaho, Montana, Minnesota, Illinois, Massachusetts, and New York. She pursued further studies at the University of Minnesota, University of Washington, and Columbia University. She also spent a summer in New York studying Americanization and earned a certificate to teach English to immigrants in the state of New York.

A former student and friend, Louise Howard, recalls Nora after her retirement, admiring a very striking red suit Louise was wearing. Perhaps reflecting on her own single status, Nora was heard to

Papyrus Club, 1929. First row: left to right: Isabelle Welty, Clara Lang, Miss Toevs, Mr. Livingston, Miss Frye, Jane Rose, Velinore Sweigle: Second row: Diana Malott, Marcia Herbert, Patricia Foster, Harriet White, Lucille Wolcott, Christine Russum, Rosemary Lovell: Third row: Dorothy Sartori, Howard Fratzke, Merritt Winans, John Farquhar, Ray Weston, Thorsten Berggren, John Austin.

wonder aloud how it might have changed the course of her life if she had worn a red suit like that when she was young.

Nora loved to travel, and during her summer vacation in 1893 attended the Chicago World's Fair. In 1897 she vacationed on Isle Royale in northern Minnesota. In 1923 she took a leave from her teaching duties for a semester and traveled in Europe, visiting many sites of literary and historical significance. At the end of her European trip she vowed to return one day, perhaps taking some of her family with her, but a second trip abroad was never to take place. In 1937, upon her retirement from teaching, Nora hoped to take her great-niece, Margaret Gray, on a world tour. However, with political tensions mounting between Japan and China, this plan was soon discarded. The following years brought the escalation of events preceding World War II—and by the time the war was over, Nora was nearing the end of her life and was so crippled with arthritis that she walked using two canes.

When she retired from teaching in 1937, Nora had said that she planned to find a new occupation in order to earn some money and that she also wanted to do some writing, but just for fun, not for publication. That winter she worked in a settlement house in New York City, later writing about her experiences there.

Nora Frye on right and her sister, Clara Frye, left, standing with Will and Jennie Frye in front of the tent in which Will and Jennie lived while building their retirement cabin, 1932.

In the early '30s when she was nearing retirement, a nephew recalls that Nora had given forty acres of the family farm, which she had purchased from her mother years earlier, to her brother, Will, and his wife, Jennie, who had suffered devastating financial losses during the depression. Will and Jennie then lived in a tent on the farm for six months while they built their small retirement cabin of scrub oak. A short time later Nora and her sister, Clara, each had a basic one-room cabin built on the farm. During three or four summers just preceding and following Nora's retirement, Nora and Clara each lived in their respective cabins on the farm, taking their meals with Will and Jennie Frye at their home nearby. It seems likely that Nora did some of her reminiscing and writing during these summers on the old homestead.

Nora continued to write about her experiences until about six months before her death in Spokane on May 12, 1946. Shortly before she died, she was also tutoring a student who

Nora Frye on right with her sister, Clara, about 1934.

Family gathering, July 7, 1935, at the Will and Jennie Frye cabin. Back, left to right: Jennie Frye, Will Frye, Nora Frye, Raymond Gray, Mary Elizabeth Gray, Ann Gray, Clara Frye Bomberger, Phyllis Frye Gray, Helen Gamm. Children, left to right: Bobby Gamm, Barbara Gamm, Charles Bomberger.

wanted to improve his writing skills in preparation for entering college.

Warm-hearted and empathetic, Nora enjoyed people and valued her relationships with them. Almost fifty years after her death, memories of Nora Frye are still very much alive with family members and former students now in their 70s and 80s who knew her as children or young adults. Relatives who were children when she visited in their homes remember her love of books and reading, art, and drama, her enjoyment of gourmet foods and dining out with friends, her sense of humor, her love of nature and picnics on the banks of the Mississippi River on the old family homestead, and rousing discussions of current affairs which took place among Nora and other adults around the family dinner table.

At a class reunion years ago her former students from the Stillwater High School Class of 1907 remembered Nora as one of the best Latin teachers in the state. And Louis Livingston, Vice Principal of Lewis and Clark High School at the time of Nora's retirement, recalls clearly Nora's skills as a peacemaker among the faculty. Accord-

Nora Frye, June 1937, leaving her classroom for the last time.

ing to Mr. Livingston, when there was dissension in the ranks at faculty meetings, Nora would often very graciously interject a humorous comment which would cause everyone to laugh, thereby clearing the air and allowing the staff to deal constructively with the issues at hand.

One of Nora's fellow teachers, Charles E. Baten, upon her retirement in 1937, wrote her a letter which reads in part:

Nora Frye, about 1943.

It is with great regret that I learn that you will terminate your connection with Lewis and Clark in June.

No small part of your charm, which you possess now and have possessed all the while, is the smile of pleasure and the sparkle of interest in your eyes whenever you speak to anyone.

I consider it an honor to have been associated with you on the faculty of Lewis and Clark High School and to have counted you as a friend.

A few weeks preceding her retirement, the orchestra at Lewis and Clark High School honored Miss Frye with a special concert. That year the *Tiger*, the yearbook at Lewis and Clark, was dedicated to her. The inscription under her photograph reads:

To Miss Nora Frye,

Whose sincere spirit of friendliness, kindly sense of humor, and sympathetic understanding have endeared her to Lewis and Clark,

Whose life work, not only in her daily classroom routine but also in countless evenings in the homes of her young friends, has been to stimulate and uplift youth in its quest for self-expression and creative power,

Whose life interprets the word "teacher" in its highest sense, is lovingly dedicated this June, 1937 *Tiger*.

On May 9, 1946 Nora finalized her will, leaving her entire estate to her sister, Clara, with whom she was living at the time. Nora had planned a summer visit to Elk River, Minnesota, but on May 12, 1946, three days after signing her will, she died of a heart attack.

Nora chose her burial place in beautiful Orono Cemetery in Elk River, Minnesota, beside a small lake, next to her parents and several of her brothers and sisters. A simple granite stone with the inscription, "Nora Frye, 1867-1946," marks her grave.

Janet Schultz Panger

Grave, Orono Cemetery, Elk River, Minnesota.